# MARKETING REVEALED

# MARKETING REVEALED

## Challenging the Myths

Willem Burgers

First published in 2008 by
PALGRAVE MACMILLAN
Houndmills, Basingstoke, Hampshire RG21 6XS and
175 Fifth Avenue, New York, N.Y. 10010
Companies and representatives throughout the world.

PALGRAVE MACMILLAN is the global academic imprint of the Palgrave
Macmillan division of St. Martin's Press, LLC and of Palgrave Macmillan Ltd.
Macmillan® is a registered trademark in the United States, United Kingdom
and other countries. Palgrave is a registered trademark in the European
Union and other countries.

ISBN-13: 978–0–230–53714–9
ISBN-10: 0–230–53714–6

This book is printed on paper suitable for recycling and made from fully
managed and sustained forest sources. Logging, pulping and manufacturing
processes are expected to conform to the environmental regulations of
the country of origin.

A catalogue record for this book is available from the British Library.

A catalog record for this book is available from the Library of Congress.

10  9  8  7  6  5  4  3  2  1
17  16  15  14  13  12  11  10  09  08

Printed and bound in Great Britain by
Cromwell Press Ltd, Trowbridge, Wiltshire

To the managers of so many different companies: thank you for the knowledge you have shared. Thank you for the trust you have placed in me. This book is not just for you, but also from you

# Contents

# Foreword

I do consulting and teach company-specific marketing programs in Asia, Europe, and the United States for a variety of global companies such as Nokia, Kodak, Sony, IBM, Motorola, GE, BASF, Electrolux, Lufthansa, and so forth, as well as Chinese companies such as Ping An, Lenovo, BBK, San Ming, Guang Ming, Jianxi Motor Company, and Zenisun.

I also have worked with smaller companies such as the Dial One franchise organization in the US, start-up companies, and even the bar across the street from what used to be my fishing camp in pre-Katrina New Orleans. So what new things, practical things, can I possibly tell and teach these managers and entrepreneurs? How do I find material that is new and interesting to my customers?

I read a lot, but I also learn from the managers I teach. They tell me what is wrong, what is true, and what is new. This is why I titled the book *Marketing Revealed*. Because I write about marketing revealed to me, and now by me. I am mostly a middleman between business people who are educating each other. This probably explains why these managers enthuse about how revealing, eye opening, practical, and immediately useful our discussions have been.

Read this book carefully and your life and career will be better, your company will be more profitable, your spouse will love you more, your stock market performance will improve – everything will be better. This is so because marketing at its core is about exchange of one thing for another thing. Marketing is about everything.

Please enjoy this book.

Willem Burgers, Ph.D.
*Bayer Chair Professor of Strategy and Marketing*
*China Europe International Business School*[1]
*Shanghai*

---

1. As a young school we still need to build our brand. The China Europe International Business School MBA has been ranked # 1 in Asia by the London *Financial Times*.

# Introduction

Do we really know marketing? In the 1980s the personal computer industry was ruled by giants: IBM, Apple, HP, and Compaq. Minor players included huge companies such as Philips, Siemens, Toshiba, Sony and others. Among them, year after year, they spent billions of dollars on R&D to improve products and production techniques. How much R&D money was spent on researching and developing new markets, or on researching and developing new marketing methods? Little if any.

Then Michael Dell defeats the whole industry. How did Michael Dell win? He didn't invent a better computer. His product was not exciting and it never has been exciting. He had no economies of scale on starting out. He had no distribution. Stores refused to sell his computer. He had to sell direct. He had hardly money for promotion and brand building. He was so poor he had to use his own last name as brand name: Dell. I think if you paid $100,000 to a brand name consulting company and they gave you "Dell" you'd ask for your money back.

So how does he win? He invents a better marketing method. He offers to fix your computer problems over the phone or otherwise come to your house or office the next day. By the mid-1980s many new computer buyers had no clue about computers. Dell's new method for delivery of product, and especially service, appealed to the emerging segment of computer-illiterate computer buyers, the so-called "rest of us." Why didn't his competitors research and try new marketing methods? This book answers that question.

Further, why didn't the major personal computer companies copy Dell? *While the engineers were tearing apart one another's computers to look for better ideas, how many marketing managers were tearing apart Michael Dell's business model?* Few if any. Did these marketing managers really know and do their job? No they did not. They played marketing manager; they impersonated a marketing manager in the same way that Frank Abagnale/Leonardo DiCaprio impersonated an airline pilot, a medical doctor, and a lawyer in the movie *Catch Me If You Can*.[1] If Frank Abagnale/Leonardo DiCaprio had impersonated a marketing manager, he would have never gotten caught.

---

1. The movie was based approximately on the even stranger real story described in the book *Catch Me If You Can* by Frank W. Abagnale, with Stan Redding, 1980, Grosset & Dunlap, New York. Read the book. You will certainly enjoy it. Then please ponder whether it is possible in your company for someone to build a successful career as a marketing manager while not knowing anything about marketing.

I am constantly surprised when working with so many different companies as to how many marketing managers have only the vaguest notion of what they are supposed to be doing. They are lucky their CEO also does not know. Does your marketing department know its job and do its job? Do you? What is the job of marketing? What do you need to know to be, rather than play, marketing manager? This book will let you find out.

I start any lecture by asking managers to listen and look for ideas they can put into action. Recently I spent a morning at Columbia University in New York talking to 30 executives about creating customer value. One participant later on was kind enough to inform me that he put down 13 ideas for action in the four hours he had listened to me. I am flattered to think that 13 ideas could come from my remarks that morning (and a bit worried for the participant's company, having maybe too much room for improvement). The fact is, however, even as few as one idea for action per day, resulting in change in your company, makes the investment of time and money in marketing education entirely worthwhile. Please look in this book for ideas you can put into action.

So have your notepad and pen ready! When you finish this book I don't want you to say: this book is one of the most entertaining and interesting books I ever read about marketing. Not that I would disagree. But that is not what I want you to say. I want you to say: this book is one of the most useful books I ever read about business ... now I will do this and that, and so forth. I want this book to change the things you do, and the way you do things, as well as the way you think about things. Let us start by taking a look at what it is, this thing called marketing.

# 1 Marketing: What It Is

## Key messages to whet your appetite

▶ When you understand, you see no differences.
▶ You must know the four Cs to use the four Ps.
▶ It is all the same P and C.
▶ You don't need problems for solutions.

## What is marketing?

*Is marketing just common sense? A friend of mine – a marketing professor – once sat on a state government board that made venture capital investments. While entrepreneurs laid out their finance or production plans, all was quiet as respective experts on the board would offer suggestions or ask questions. But whenever the discussion turned to the marketability or marketing of the product, suddenly everybody joined enthusiastically in the discussion. Everybody was an expert in marketing.*

*Why is everybody an expert? Because it is widely believed marketing is just applied common sense. Unfortunately, common sense is the least common of senses. Everybody has his or her own common sense. But if marketing is not common sense, then what is it?*

*One way to answer this question is to say that marketing is what marketing managers do, or should do. Looking at the question in that way, we can say that marketing is the famous four Ps and Cs. We can then also say that many companies do not have marketing and that many marketing managers do not do marketing and that, more likely, nobody rather than everybody is an expert. Chapter 1 explores these ideas.*

1

# The famous four Ps and Cs:
# a brief history

Prior to the 1960s, marketing textbooks typically were organized by product. Chapter 1 would be "Marketing of Consumer Products," Chapter 2 "Marketing of Industrial Products," Chapter 3 "Marketing of Services," Chapter 4 "Marketing of Agricultural Products," and so forth. Then, one morning, Professor E. Jerome McCarthy woke up and realized that it was the same, in all the chapters, there was always a Product, a Place, a Price, and Promotion. So he invented the now-famous four Ps marketing mix, rendering all prior textbooks obsolete. He made many millions of dollars selling his textbook.[1]

McCarthy's invention reflects a general truth: that differences are easy to see but underneath those differences everything is often the same. The ancient Greeks – the philosophers Leucippos and Demokritos in the fifth century BC – reasoned that if you cut down water or sand or meat into smaller and smaller portions, ultimately, just before you end up with nothing, you end up with identical small pieces holding onto one another in different ways, indivisible pieces the Greeks called "atoms."

So it is in marketing – cut long enough and it is all the same little pieces holding onto one another in different ways. For example, the difference between consumer marketing and industrial marketing is that consumers buy products for their own satisfaction while industrial buyers buy products as components in a larger product to satisfy customers down the line. But consider a cosmetics company that discovers spending on cosmetics drops off after marriage. Why is that?

Maybe women buy cosmetics as a component in a larger product to satisfy their own customers (men) and decide, not unreasonably, that in the more monopolistic arrangement called marriage, investments in customer satisfaction can be reduced. I have not seen any research, but probably men buy fewer flowers after marriage. Seen this way, the cosmetics and flower business are sort of business-to-business too, helping customers satisfy customers' customers.

Alternatively, consider a company buying a new Lear jet, selecting mahogany panelling for the new boardroom, donating money to the opera. Are those expenditures meant to satisfy the company's customers' needs?

Once we realize that everything is always the same, we can learn from the successes of not only our competitors in our own industry, *but from the successes of any company in any industry*. Small companies or large companies, consumer or industrial, domestic or foreign, goods or services, any company can learn from any company. Likely, the most interesting things can be learned from companies that are least like our own companies.

*You can learn from the successes of any company in any industry.*

## Ps or Cs? Ps and Cs!

Many have tried to add Ps such as "Probe" or "People" or "Physical evidence" to McCarthy's four Ps framework. Record holder, I think, is Professor Jerry Wind, who in 1986[2] proposed "The Eleven Ps of Marketing" – but for the most part the four Ps still rule in marketing today.

However, Bob Lauterborn, James L. Knight professor of advertising at the University of North Carolina, offers a very different critique of marketing's main framework. He points out that the four Ps reflect the marketing manager's point of view even as marketing admonishes one and all to take the customer's point of view. In other words, marketing's main framework ignores marketing's main message.

Lauterborn therefore suggests the four Cs to replace the four Ps, arguing that the four Ps reflect the producer's point of view, while his four Cs reflect the customer's point of view.[3] Specifically, Lauterborn suggests we should look at the following:

▶ Consumer wants and needs instead of Product
▶ Convenience instead of Place
▶ Cost instead of Price
▶ Communication instead of Promotion

The idea is that Convenience, for example, is a better term than Place since it focuses on a customer benefit. However, convenience can be created not only by place, but also by product (for example, making the package easy to open), or price (for example, $5.00 is a more convenient price than $5.07), or promotion (for example, putting a map in a yellow pages advertisement). Still, it makes a lot of sense to think about convenience.

Similarly, it makes a lot of sense to think about cost to the customer rather than just price. To quote Lauterborn:

Dollars are only one part of cost. What you're selling against if you're selling hamburgers is not just another burger for a few cents more or less. It's the cost of the time to drive to your place, the cost of conscience to eat meat at all, perhaps versus the cost of not treating the kids. Value is no longer the biggest burger for the cheapest price.

Lauterborn is right. Sometimes even a zero-dollar price may be too high. A few years ago, I bought a so-called "Select Edition" Jaguar from the Jaguar dealer in New Orleans. The car was two years old but supposedly had been checked out carefully.[4] The car had to be returned to the shop time and again to fix the same problems. The dealer would cheerfully tell me to "Just bring the car in. We'll see what it is this time."

The dealer never considered that returning the car, waiting around for the loaner, coming back for the car again – about once every other month – represented a huge cost. Sure, the price of repairs was zero, but the cost was still too high. So I sued to force Jaguar to take the car and give me my money back (I settled for a cash payment of $5,000). I also decided never to buy anything from Ford, Jaguar, or this dealer again. Cost is not simply price.

Michael Dell, in contrast, significantly lowered the cost of owning a personal computer by agreeing to stop by your house or office to do repairs. He eliminated the customer's cost of disconnecting the computer, then transporting the computer, then waiting for weeks without a computer, then re-transporting the computer, then reconnecting the computer, then finding out the computer was not fixed after all. Have his competitors learned from him? Here is a little update, twenty (!) years later, from Geek.com[5] on some of the most respected names in the industry:

> Toshiba now contracts all repair work to centers that take as long as six weeks, parts are now handled by third parties …
> … Once they [Sony] are out of warranty, you will find it very difficult to find parts. Repairs take weeks or even months …

With competitors like that, Dell has been pretty safe against even his own recent marketing blunders (those we will bring up later). There has been a trend for a number of years toward "experiential" marketing, meaning we should try to market "consumption experiences" rather than "products." Lauterborn's four Cs dovetail nicely with this trend. It is not that Dell is better than say Toshiba; it is the experience of owning a Dell that is more pleasant than the experience of owning a Toshiba. Similarly, that Jaguar dealer in New Orleans looks at the car he sold me and thinks it is a nice car, ignoring the horrible experience of owning the car.

Lauterborn's four Cs are the experiential counterpart of McCarthy's four Ps. Therefore, we should not replace our marketing mix of tools (the four Ps) with a marketing mix of customer experiences (the four Cs). We should look at both.

*Marketing tools (Ps) translate into customer experiences (Cs).*

## Marketing principles hold across industries

Since the four Ps and Cs are what we might call the atomic structure of marketing – regardless of industry – the principles and ideas behind success in one industry should apply in every industry. Is everything always the same? Michael Dell has expressed doubts that his direct selling and servicing model would work outside the PC industry. With all due respect, I must disagree.

Dell does home delivery of his product and service. That idea also created the Domino's Pizza chain. And the lower costs for the customer meant lower costs also for Domino's, which expanded into many areas through home delivery without building any restaurants (not a minor saving if you are a restaurant).

Home delivery of service also works for Carl Sewell, a car dealer with $1 billion in sales (that is a very big car dealer). As Sewell tells us in his excellent book:[6] "Let's say it's five in the morning, [you are at home] and you discover you have a flat … You call and the service technician will drive over … and take care of you." Carl Sewell does not charge to fix your tire at five in the morning or to bring you a new key if you break your key off in your lock late at night at the airport. He says he can't charge since only friends will come out to save you in the middle of the night, and friends are not supposed to charge friends. So how does this extravagant generosity save him money? Another quote:

> Let's say it costs $25 to go over and let that customer into his car. Think about the cost of a radio ad. In Dallas, during peak drive times, a 60-second commercial on a popular station costs $700. For the $25 we spent letting you into your car, I probably have a customer for life. How many customers for life am I going to get from a $700 radio ad? I'd need 28 – $700 divided by 28 equals $25 – to get the same results from the ad that I got from helping that customer … Common sense tells me we're not going to get 28 customers for life from one radio commercial.

*One way or another, making your customer's life easier saves you money.*

# It's all the same P (or C)

Sewell makes an enormously important point here. He erases the dividing line between Place and Promotion strategy. He talks about good service and radio commercials as interchangeable!

His delivery of service to the customer wherever and whenever the customer needs him is a part of his Place strategy. One might think that the delivery of service in the middle of the night at no charge makes his Place strategy more expensive. But in Sewell's way of thinking it is a very cost-effective Promotion strategy. The important point here is that whether a P is Place, Price, Product, Promotion depends on your perspective. Here, from Sewell's perspective, free service delivered to your home is not Price, Product and Place – it is Promotion.

A friend of mine in Michigan bought a large house subdivided into five two-room efficiencies, each with its own cooking and bathroom facilities. But the small, low-priced apartments attracted undesirable tenants. He spent all his time and money fighting with tenants and repairing vandalism. In despair, he evicted all the tenants, wanting to change the house back into a single family home. I suggested he advertise the units in the newspaper under the heading "rooms" rather than "apartments." Now he has the most expensive rooms in town and rents to people working in the city, with families and homes too far away to make a daily commute. His Product was the problem, but redefining the product through changing Promotion was the solution, the much cheaper solution.

A small travel agency in New Orleans focused on Spanish-speaking customers. How could it distinguish its travel agency from the others? As a general rule, there is no difference in tickets or prices from one travel agency to the other. To differentiate its product, this agency advertised on the local Spanish language radio station, offering financing of plane tickets to visit back home through a layaway plan. Customers send in a fixed amount each month and in one or two years the customers receive their tickets.

This approach proved so successful that Mr Schneider, the founder of the agency, soon bought the very radio station on which he had started his advertising. Thus, the best product differentiation strategy may be a different pricing strategy.

> *A problem and its solution need not exist in the same "P" dimension.*

## Marketing's four strategies

I suggest therefore that companies adopt the framework below to guide their marketing mix decisions. This merged framework recognizes explicitly that investments in any of the four Ps will impact all four Cs. By thinking of the impact of investment in any P on any C we can counteract one serious longstanding criticism of the four Ps, namely, that the so-called four P marketing mix is a contradiction in terms because the four P framework un-mixes the marketing mix, separating functions that should be applied in an integrated fashion.

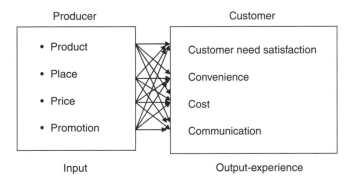

If a group discussion in a company gets too heavily focused on problems the company faces, I ask managers to forget about the problems and to go through the four Ps one by one. I ask them to try to determine for each of the four Ps changes that will improve any of the four Cs.

It is interesting to see how many ideas emerge to solve problems once we ignore problems and just look for solutions. Perhaps this is because when we search for solutions without problems, we are more likely to look in directions no one else is looking, more likely to be creative. The essence of creative art, after all, is the solution without a problem. Like a new song – no one needed to hear that great new song until its creation.

Another reason that so many ideas emerge is that companies normally associate R&D with inventing new products and new production methods, not with inventing new markets or new marketing methods. The 4P-4C framework above offers also a convenient handle for thinking about marketing R&D, the topic of the next chapter.

*You don't need problems before you look for solutions.*

---

✍   **POINTS TO REMEMBER**

☞ **You can learn from the successes of any company in any industry.**
☞ **Marketing tools (Ps) translate into customer experiences (Cs).**
☞ **One way or another, making your customer's life easier saves you money.**
☞ **A problem and its solution need not exist in the same "P" dimension.**
☞ **You don't need problems before you look for solutions.**

---

## Notes

1. J. McCarthy, *Basic Marketing: A Managerial Approach*, 1st edn (Irwin, 1960). Others had proposed the idea of a marketing mix before. But they didn't package their idea as well. Marketing matters.
2. In a speech during the May 1986 International Curriculum and Language Development Seminar at the Wharton School.
3. R. Lauterborn, "New Marketing Litany: 4Ps Passe; C words take over," *Advertising Age* (1 October, 1990), p. 26.
4. I should have realized that buying a "Select Edition" used car from a dealer is a good way to get stuck with a recycled lemon. After all, people prefer to trade a lemon back to a dealer, rather than sell it to friends or family, or to a stranger who might come back to yell at them.
5. http://www2.geek.com/discus/messages/27/67378.html?1151307533
6. Carl Sewell and Paul B. Brown, *Customers For Life*, rev. edn (Currency, 2002). This is definitely one of the very best books ever written on business. A long-time bestseller that is strongly recommended by everybody who is anybody in business, including CEOs and chairmen of companies such as Wal-Mart, Pepsico, GM, and so on.

# 2  Marketing R&D

## Key messages to whet your appetite

▶ Is your marketing manager killing you?
▶ Your R&D budget and allocation need fixing.
▶ Love your pink computer guy!
▶ Embrace continuous experimentation.

## No marketing R&D

*When companies have a marketing manager who only "plays" marketing manager then there will be little or no marketing R&D. It is astonishing how whole industries will display a complete lack of marketing R&D without anyone in the industry thinking much if anything is amiss. R&D simply is not part of marketing's job description in some industries.*

*What do we mean by marketing R&D? Why do so many industries, companies, and managers shy away from marketing R&D, if they are even aware of the possibilities of marketing R&D? Marketing R&D can be as simple as checking if pink might be a good color to help differentiate your PCs, sell more of your PCs, sell your PCs at a higher price. Marketing R&D can be as complicated as trying to figure out why so many heart disease patients risk their own lives discontinuing the use of statins, a drug with few or no side effects with proven significant effect on reducing mortality.*

*Why is marketing R&D such an underdeveloped activity in many industries? Four explanations: 1. managers don't know what marketing R&D is; 2. managers decide that to engage in marketing R&D is unhealthy for one's career; 3. managers hate any ideas they did not think of; 4. managers are brainwashed by "the tyranny of benchmarking, consulting firms, and analysts."[1]*

*What can be done to develop a marketing R&D capability in your company? Awareness of what is not done and of what could be done is crucial. Offering everyone in your company a copy of this chapter might be a very good idea.*

## The PC industry

Let us continue first the earlier example of the PC industry. European companies had plenty of time to admire Dell's success and to marvel at the damage he was inflicting on bigger and richer rivals. Unfortunately, none of these European companies possessed the "intellectual infrastructure" to try Dell's methods in Europe. All waited around patiently for Dell to come and try his methods in Europe.

Of course, these companies knew very well what Dell was doing in the United States. But their marketing managers also were convinced that Dell's model would not work in Europe. These managers had no clue, and their CEOs had no clue, that marketing's job was to *find* ways to make the Dell model work in Europe. So they waited quietly for their day of execution. Dell came, tried, made what proved to be only minor adjustments, proved the nay-sayers wrong, and put the European personal computer companies out of their misery. According to Michael Dell: "The message was always the same: 'Our country is different. Your business model won't work here' ... To be sure, we do some localization ... some Germans aren't comfortable telephoning ... they will, however, respond to a fax number."[2]

These companies had big marketing departments and experienced marketing managers. At least they thought they did. But in too many companies and too many industries, R&D is not part of marketing's job description, and the people in charge of marketing don't know that it should be.

> *Identify the world's most successful companies; study their marketing; modify to suit you.*

Was ignoring Dell's tremendous success and his imminent arrival a special case? I am afraid not. It took nearly two decades, and the return of Steve Jobs – outsider always – before anyone finally thought of trying colors other than ugly office yellow, office grey, or off-white or black for personal computers. A whole industry, numerous companies, hundreds of senior marketing managers, thousands of junior marketing managers, plenty of marketing consultants, complaining for two decades about commoditization, price-sensitive customers, price erosion, attending industry conferences and seminars, studying mega trends and hiring consumer psychology consultants, never thinking to see if personal computers might be improved through personalization.

Do you need a Ph.D. in marketing to think of using nice colors? Nice colors worked for selling more cars and phones. "Cars and phones are different." I can hear a marketing manager somewhere say it. I hope for your sake that it is not your marketing manager.

Apple gained several points of market share by introducing its iMac computers several years ago in different translucent colors such as green and orange. Why, before Apple finally did, did no other company think to try this? Our engineers work every day thinking of new and different things to try; many of our marketing managers don't.

Apple's translucent colors were not copied by its competitors (no surprise there). Following on the iMac computers' success, however, translucent colors became popular in some surprising new places such as garden tools.[3] As said: any company can learn from any other company in any other industry.

I imagine many managers working in the PC industry use laptops. Best Buy's Geek Squad founder has figured out something these many managers have never discovered: "The biggest customer disappointment is the time it takes to fix a laptop."[4] It still takes three to four weeks today to repair a laptop. (What do PC companies do with all these laptops for all those weeks? Do they look at them? Drive around with them in a truck?) How much R&D money has the industry spent looking for ways to reduce the ridiculously long repair time? Maybe they have never looked because managers in the industry use their company's IT department to repair their laptops within one day.

Best Buy now will assume responsibility for repairs, thereby further commoditizing the manufacturers, slashing turn-around time to no more than three days: one day for shipping, one day for fixing, one day for shipping back. Is this logistically too complex for the manufacturers?

*Marketing can have simple solutions for big problems. But you have to want to look.*

## Are people just bags of chemicals?

The pharmaceutical industry has a similar tradition of very limited attention to non-product features such as brand name, product shape, size, color, and so on. This is not because such features are not important. The efficacy of medicine depends substantially on patient's belief in the medicine. Such belief can be enhanced by careful attention to non-product features. But the industry focuses on R&D, and R&D focuses on products and production.

In the non-prescription pharmaceutical market we may see a few brand names that convey a message. For example, there is Alleve for your head-ache. More often, names reflect obscure technical details. Diane 35, for example, is a women's contraceptive that also eliminates acne. The target market for this product is young women, especially young women with acne. But the "35" implies that the product is for a Diane who is nearer to the age of 35, rather than 21. So what does the "35" stand for? It refers to the 35mg of ethinyl estradiol (???) in the product. This sort of thing serves as an entertaining example in a marketing seminar, but rings no bells and raises no eyebrows in a pharmaceutical company.

Further, with pharmaceuticals the efficacy of the product depends on patients taking the product faithfully and appropriately, for example, with or without food, and with or without water. When patients receive instructions to take a pill once a day, they might ask whether to take it in the morning or evening. The doctor might respond that it doesn't matter. It doesn't matter if patients are merely bags of chemicals. But in fact patients are decision-making bags of chemicals. Possibly, patients are more likely to take the product faithfully if they are instructed to take it in the morning after they brush their teeth. This way, the taking of the drug is connected to an established daily habit.

One major reason for lost sales in the industry is premature discontinu-ation of a drug by patients. Cholesterol-reducing statins are discontinued by half of all patients within one year and by some 70 percent within two years.[5] Research on how to help patients take their drugs, how to make taking a drug a daily habit, would benefit not merely the many patients who now die prematurely, it would help the industry. There might be a few billion dollars of lost revenues and profits here. I have seen only very recently any signs that the industry is interested in this sort of research questions. It is not ill will, or disinterest in patients, or incompetence that causes this industry failure. It is simply that the industry does not look beyond the factory gate. They are focused on the product and produc-tion, not on the market and marketing. Therefore, they focus on what happens inside the company, not on what happens outside the company.

*What happens with your product once it has left your building? Do R&D.*

## It is not lonely at the bottom

The PC industry and the pharmaceutical industry are not alone. Airlines similarly have no interest in what happens with you after you get off the plane. Airlines could make leaflets available with information on local transportation options, perhaps with warnings on the various scams by local taxi operators. But they spend their energy on what happens on the plane rather than what happens after you get off the plane. Once I had a six-hour wait at an airport *after* my flight. I was refused access to the business lounge. I was told I had already completed my trip. When that nice stewardess and smiling pilot say bye-bye when you leave the plane, they are serious.

It is not that the industry doesn't want to help you. They can't help you because they have not hired anyone in marketing to help you, and they don't know they should. They can't help themselves either. Professor Jeffrey Pfeffer from Stanford University points out that Southwest Airlines has been America's best-performing stock from 1974 through 2004. Accordingly, he asks: "Why did it take 24 years for someone to copy the Southwest model?"[6] Good question. The answer is simple: the airlines haven't hired anyone in marketing to help the airlines either.

*Have at least a few real marketing people in your company.*

I asked a leading chemical company, spending well in excess of 1 billion euros on R&D every year, how much of the money is spent on marketing and market R&D. Managers were not sure of what marketing and market R&D would entail. I ask marketing managers simple questions all the time to prove to them how little they know about markets and marketing for their own products. Who sells more for you: tall salespeople or short salespeople? Marketing managers don't know. If the purchasing manager is a woman, should you send a male or a female sales person? What if the purchasing manager is a man? Marketing managers don't know. Should you use one person in your ad to talk to your customer, or two, or more? Marketing managers don't know. The ad on which you plan to spend US$50 million over the next six months; does the target audience understand the message, will the target audience become more likely to buy after they have seen the ad, will the target audience realize that this ad is by your company and for your product? Fifty-five of the 100 largest advertisers in the United States have no idea. They don't pre-test advertisements prior to running the full advertising campaign.[7]

Companies spend a lot of money on market research and some of that money is well spent. But market research is not the same as marketing R&D. Market research is mostly outsourced to market research companies and focuses on finding answers to questions where we know we don't have the answers. A significant proportion of market research also is done when we know the answers, but we need to blame somebody in case our decisions don't work out.

Partially because market research is mostly outsourced, we do not innovate. We pay market researchers to bring us answers, not to bring us new questions. This is really too bad when there are so many unasked interesting questions: is pink a good color for a computer? Should repair service be delivered to the customer's house? Will patients more likely stick with their medicine if we tell them to take it in the morning? Such marketing innovation questions, both obvious and non-obvious, are asked by not nearly enough companies.

> *Look for questions to ask.*

## Is avoiding marketing R&D a safer career choice?

Ignorance of marketing is not the only explanation for this amazing industry-wide lack of trying simple things that can make a huge difference. Having met some very smart managers I find that an equally powerful explanation is Kenneth Galbraith's dictum: "In any great organization it is far, far safer to be wrong with the majority than to be right alone."[8]

Only making unique mistakes is really costly. Suppose you suggest selling a pink computer. Suppose your idea fails. The pink computer does not sell. You will be known forever in your company as the "pink computer guy." When you make a new suggestion, you will hear soft whispers: "another pink computer idea." Marketing can only find the way by trying different ways, by making mistakes. You don't want your accountants to try different things and make lots of mistakes. But for your marketing managers, making mistakes must be mandatory. Ask yourself therefore this question: are marketing managers in your company encouraged to experiment and try all sorts of new and different ideas?

When we look exclusively in one direction, we are bound to miss the blindingly obvious sitting in another direction. When we only look for innovation in the technical sphere of product and production, we are certain to miss innovation opportunities in markets and marketing. Sometimes, as in the case of Apple's colors, the blindingly obvious is a missed opportunity. Sometimes, as in the case of Dell, the blindingly obvious is a killer cement truck headed our way with headlights blazing.

There is some concern these days that innovation itself is now commoditized, that innovation merely suffices to keep you in the game. Professor Collins, in his famous book *Good to Great*,[9] reports his findings that technological innovation does not distinguish great companies from good companies. This does not mean that technological innovation is not important. It means that technological innovation is not enough. We need to go beyond technological innovation. We need to embrace also marketing innovation, especially in technically oriented industries where the very idea of market and marketing innovation is often absent. We need to make it safe, and mandatory, for marketing managers to try new things.

> *Don't let marketing R&D be a career killer.*

## What to do?

So how can companies escape their product and production focus, and expand the firm's R&D focus to include markets and marketing? How do we look for innovation in markets and marketing? How do we look outside rather than only inside our company? My answer to that question is by way of integration of marketing's four Ps and four Cs and by assigning marketing managers the specific responsibility to search for new ideas and try new ideas, especially new ideas that cross marketing's four Ps silos. I cited Dell, Carl Sewell and Domino's Pizza as examples. We will look at additional examples in chapters following.

But tools and talent are not the only issues. Galbraith tells us that managers prefer to make the same mistakes everyone makes. Pfeffer tells us that managers suffer under "the tyranny of benchmarking, consulting firms, and analysts" offering all managers everywhere the same suggestions. I suspect managers suffer under this tyranny because it serves them well. Managers get to make the same mistakes everybody makes, as well as make these same mistakes upon the recommendation of expensive consultants.

I think we need foremost company-wide awareness of what is meant by marketing R&D, company-wide acceptance that only nine out of ten ideas we try may work, company-wide reverence for ideas worth trying out, rather than skepticism because most ideas tried won't work, and company-wide awareness that the CEO is very serious about marketing doing its job and very serious about getting rid of those who will sacrifice the company on the altar of temporary job safety. Culture is the greatest bottleneck. As I mentioned in the opening section: copy this chapter and spread it through your company!

*Copy this Chapter and spread it through your company.*

While crossing silo boundaries can help eliminate longstanding frustrations and aggravations across functions such as sales and service and promotion, and so on, not everybody will be ecstatic. Company group discussions using the 4P-4C framework to attack problems and suggest solutions can be fruitful, and they can also antagonize the responsible manager. After all, if someone else thinks of a workable solution, why didn't this responsible manager think of it in the first place?

I recently worked with a company that produces digital televisions. In a discussion I discovered that repairs of digital TVs in some geographical areas could take as long as six weeks. I suggested that any time a repair takes more than four weeks, you have permanently lost that one customer for that product, plus any other products you sell – and all the other customers to whom your ex-customer tells his tale of woe.

I suggested one idea to fix this problem: "You know about loaner cars – offer loaner TVs." The manager objects that because they had several different models, this would be a logistical nightmare. I responded that car dealers offer loaners and nobody expects to get the exact make or model. He responded that digital TVs are not the same as cars: "Our business is different." (This statement is frequently the last refuge of the incompetent.)

The other managers, smelling blood maybe, weighed in with their own suggestions. The more suggestions came about – concentrating sales to fewer outlets, a gift of cash, a free movie – the more energetically the responsible manager rejected any and all of them. His face was red, and I detected a distinct resentment for me in his eyes.

I might have sarcastically commented that it was nice to see his great passion on this problem, now that it had become expressly his problem rather than just a problem for the company's customers. But working too hard on humiliating my customers would not be good marketing or good service on my part. So instead I suggested we write down the different ideas for the service manager to evaluate costs versus benefits, thereby returning the problem to its rightful owner.

I suspect marketing managers hate to admit that somebody else saw a way where they saw none. Engineers typically welcome input and love learning from competitors. Marketing managers often behave in opposite fashion. Don't allow your marketing managers to behave in this fashion. The behavior may be natural. But it is too costly.

> *The willingness to see, try, and embrace solutions is scarce.*

---

### ✍ POINTS TO REMEMBER

- ☞ Identify the world's most successful companies; study their marketing; modify to suit you.
- ☞ Marketing can have simple solutions for big problems. But you have to want to look.
- ☞ What happens with your product once it has left your building? Do R&D.
- ☞ Have at least a few real marketing people in your company.
- ☞ Look for questions to ask.
- ☞ Don't let marketing R&D be a career killer.
- ☞ Copy this chapter and spread it through your company.
- ☞ The willingness to see, try, and embrace solutions is scarce.

---

## Notes

1. Jeffrey Pfeffer, the Thomas D. Dee Professor of Organizational Behavior at Stanford University's Graduate School of Business offers the "tyranny" explanation in his article, "Dare to Be Different," *Business 2.0* (September 2004), p. 94.
2. Michael Dell with Catherine Fredman, *Direct from Dell: Strategies that Revolutionized an Industry* (HarperCollins, 2000), pp. 28–30.

3. Stacy Downs, "Green's for grass, not for hoses," www.azstarnet.com (11 January 2004).
4. Nicole Maestri, "Best Buy's Geek Squad steps up laptop repair," *USA Today* (22 October 2006).
5. Richard S. Safeer and Cynthia L. Lacivita, "Choosing Drug Therapy for Patients with Hyperlipidemia," *American Family Physician* (1 June 2000), p. 1.
6. Pfeffer, "Dare to be Different," p. 58.
7. According to a 2001 study by Ipsos-ASI: "Copy Testing U.S.-Style," www.ipsos-ideas.com, (23 August, 2003).
8. John Kenneth Galbraith, *The Guardian* (London: 28 July 1989).
9. Jim Collins, *Good to Great: Why Some Companies Make the Leap ... and Others Don't* (Collins, 2001).

# 3 Marketing as a Philosophy of Business

**Key messages to whet your appetite**

▶ Nobody loves you like you do
▶ You can't see yourself, but you should try
▶ Suffer like you make your customers suffer

## The Tao of marketing

*During dinner a friend once asked me: "Willem, what would you say is the Tao of marketing?" I had to think about that. "What is the Tao of Tao?" I first asked. Having given the question some thought, my best answer would be that the Tao of marketing, its core idea, is the ability to see through our customers' eyes, the ability to take the customer's perspective.*

*Unfortunately, seeing through our customers' eyes is impossible. To see what our customers see we have to not know what they do not know. This is impossible. We always know more than our customers about our company and our product.*

*One reason we see so many advertisements that only make sense to the advertiser is exactly because the advertiser already knows what the advertisement means to say. The advertiser knows too much. Just like with a riddle, once you see the solution it becomes hard to imagine why other people can't see it. That's why we have this problem seeing what our customers are seeing. We cannot "unknow" what we know.*

*Fortunately, marketing is like playing golf. We do not need a perfect score to win. We only need a better score than our competition. Even Tiger Woods will never hit 18 holes in one. So how do we improve our customer perspective*

19

*score? This chapter suggests six exercises. These exercises do not solve problems; they do not build our business; they do not reduce our costs. These exercises increase the probability we will make the right decisions by looking at reality through our customers' eyes.*

## Where is the value of a company?

Marketing holds that the *value of the assets of a company rests on its customers.* Oil reserves, for example, count today as assets, but they were worthless until customers wanted oil and they will be worthless once again when customers no longer want oil. Without customers, a company's book value is mostly a fiction or historical artifact. This is why companies must view their business from the perspective of their customers. In marketing we know that good things happen to people who have good customers.

Human resources think differently. HR thinks people make a company. In other words, good things happen to people who hire good people. I once heard a senior manager (with an HR background) respond to a skeptical question about his company's market entry strategy by stating that he had plans to hire the best people, pay them well, build them into sharp and focused teams, and so forth. Marketing thinks that good people come to good things. If the company's marketing strategy is flawed, good people will be too smart to join or stay.

Finance thinks differently, too. Stock analysts, for example, try to maintain good relationships with top managers of the companies they follow; they don't want to be "frozen out." Marketing thinks stock analysts should maintain good relationships with key customers of the companies they follow, that a customer's perspective on a company is more revealing than the perspective offered by that company's managers. Peter Lynch, who built the hugely successful Magellan mutual fund, famously relied on the enthusiastic satisfaction of customers in deciding which stocks to buy and sell.[1] Taking the customers' perspective rather than the CEO perspective to judge the value of a company paid off very well for Peter Lynch and his investors.

*The value of a company rests on its customers.*

# Taking the customer perspective is not the rule

Unfortunately, taking the customer perspective appears to be the exception. Companies talk a good game about being "customer-driven." They mouth the slogans, hang up the banners, and make beautiful mission and vision statements that put the customer front and center. Then life continues as usual.

Banks open after you go to work and close before you get off work. This is inconvenient for almost anybody who works for a living – except the people who work for banks. This explains why worldwide banks have only very reluctantly – and minimally – embraced the idea of opening for business at times that are convenient for the customers.

My bank in Holland listed various time-consuming transactions that would not be performed during lunch hours. I assumed the reason for this policy might be that lunch hour naturally is very busy. Always interested to test my assumptions, I asked the teller for an explanation. "Because some of our tellers are away on lunch," she informed me.

When I do consultation or teaching for a cellular phone company, I am always one of the few people present, if not the only one, who has shopped and paid for a phone or paid a phone bill. Everybody who is anybody in a cellular phone company gets a phone for free. The model depends on your level in the company, and the monthly bill is paid, too.

Car company CEOs do not shop or pay for cars, they do not keep a lemon, they do not drop off a car at the dealer. Bill Gates does not waste his time deciphering his own error messages. Running shoe company execs get all the running shoes they want – made by their own company – for free.

Many senior managers have zero true-to-life consumption experience with their product and service. The more important the decisions you make, the less likely it is that you encounter the uncooperative warehouse manager, the torturous phone system, the baffling computer information system, or the infuriating finance department. And the less likely it is that you shop for your product or pay for your product.

A lack of customer perspective leads companies to make plans and pronouncements that to any outside observer are plain ludicrous. For example, according to Ron Zarrella in 2000, then GM's North American president: "By 2002, Cadillac should be recognized in North America as the preeminent luxury brand."[2] Only someone deep inside GM could utter such a bold impossibility in public with a straight face and without blushing. Despite its great design, even shyly imitated by the 2007 Toyota Camry, Cadillac is not now among the top three luxury brands and won't be in the discernible future.

> *It is hard to see what your customers see if you live in a different world.*

This inside perspective causes the "People Love Us" disease. So many people have bought our product X. They love us. They surely can't wait to buy product Y from us, too. The disease infected three video game companies in a row. Atari was a hugely successful video game company during the late 1970s and early 1980s. Atari then decided to produce a personal computer and name it the Atari 800 or Atari 2000. I assume you didn't buy one. Not many people did.

Nintendo dreamed that it could build on its loyal customer base in the United States to upgrade its equipment and offer home banking services. There was even some concern in Congress about implications of Japanese control of banking by America's households. It hasn't happened yet and you can stop holding your breath.

Sony too believed the next stage in its PlayStation success would be home banking services or TV watching services and whatnot. Dream on, Sony. Perhaps Sony and GM could do a little trade here. Sony could explain the difference between Cadillacs and preeminent luxury cars to GM, and GM could explain the difference between PlayStations and banking services to Sony.[3]

> *Nobody loves you like you do.*

Ludicrous ideas, unhappy customers, and missed opportunities are the cost of not taking the customer's perspective, of not feeling the customer's pain. Great companies can undo their success by losing touch with the customer. Dell has not done well in recent years. Customers have become very price-sensitive according to Michael Dell. Maybe, dear Michael, only price sensitive customers are still buying your products.

What happened with Dell's great opportunity to take advantage of HP and Compaq's difficult merger? Following the merger, in order to protect its printer sales through retailers, HP was kind enough to tamp down Compaq's big effort to follow Dell's direct sales model. Market share went down for the combined companies.[4]

What happened was a decision to reward Dell customer service representatives on the basis of calls handled per day![5] Typical wait times soared to 30 minutes as customers had to call back again and again for the same problem. Repurchase intentions for Dell customers went down.

In early 2007 "I hate Dell" scored 12,200 hits on Googlefight[6] (versus IBM 875; HP 580; Toshiba 756 and, last but not least, Sony with an amazing 26,900).

How could anyone be in a somewhat senior position at Dell and be unaware of Gateway's near-suicide in 1998 by, you guessed it, changing to a system where customer service representatives were paid on the basis of the number of calls handled per day? When Gateway denied bonuses to workers spending too much time with customers:

> Workers began doing just about anything to get customers off the phone: pretending the line wasn't working, hanging up, or often–at great expense–sending them new parts or computers. Not surprisingly, Gateway's customer satisfaction rates, once the best in the industry, fell below average. What's more, many customers stopped recommending Gateway to their friends and families; Gateway's referral business, once 50 percent of total sales, fell to about 30 percent.[7]

Co-CEOs Dell and Rollins must not have known about Gateway. They also must not have known about Cox Cable. Cable companies in the U.S. have captured some 8 percent of phone revenues. But Cox Cable captures nearly 20 percent of customers in its markets. A *Business Week* article explains:

> What is Cox's advantage? … Rather than pushing agents to hurry customers off the phone and causing multiple call-backs, Cox strives to handle issues in a single call and grades reps on how well they eliminate problems, field technicians tap into the same system used by call center reps. Cox has even started a "geek quad" to help customers with tech issues, whether they involve its gear or not.[8]

Reminds me, not, of my call to Samsung when the DVDs produced by its DVR would play neither on my Apple nor on my Sony. The Samsung service rep suggested that I call Apple and Sony. Good suggestion. Push the problem onto another company. But a better suggestion was to exchange the DVR at the store for a different one.

It is expensive not to take the customer perspective, not to undergo the wasted time and frustrations you impose on your customers. Gateway found out. Dell found out. Samsung may find out too.

Imagine that Michael Dell and his co-CEO Kevin Rollins had been forced to use the Dell customer support system any time they had PC trouble. They don't use that system, of course, since their time, as opposed to the time of the people who send them money, is too valuable.

But imagine they had waited just once for more than 30 minutes before getting a human on the phone, just to be treated to a fake answer such as: "Reformat the hard drive and then call us back if that does not work. Thank you for your call. Please feel free to call back if you have any other questions." Would Dell have continued its policy of wasting hours of customers' time just to save a few dollars, meanwhile losing big through lost sales and reduced prices? I don't think so. I think if either one had felt the customers' pain, they would have called in whoever was in charge of customer service and ordered an immediate end to the senseless and counter-productive torture.[9]

I'm sure that Dell and Rollins are very smart guys, but it is very hard to address pain you don't feel. They didn't know what they needed to know because they failed to put themselves in the customers' shoes. Not taking the customers' perspective is like driving with a blindfold on. Sooner or later you will do serious damage to others and to yourself. Here are some ways to remove the blindfold.

> *Feel your customers' pain.*

## Six ways to taking the customer's perspective

*1) Surround yourself with reality.* I delivered once the results of a marketing research project to the CEO of a consumer goods company. Sitting in his office I saw beautiful glass display cases with the requisite little spotlights and mirrors showcasing the company's products. I pointed out to him that whenever his eyes drift to the beautiful glass cases he is uneducating himself. Consumers see a plethora of products, with his products taking up at best 15 percent of the space in his product category. Some of the competitors' products look remarkably like his products.

I asked him to do me a favor and replace the glass cases with a typical supermarket shelf displaying both his products and the competition's products. He followed my advice. Now when he looks up he sees reality. I think this will improve his judgment a great deal. It also won't hurt when his marketing managers know that the boss knows and wants to know reality.

> *Surround yourself with reality.*

*2) Talk to your ex-customers.* Listen to what they tell you. Find out why they left you. Unhappy ex-customers won't make you feel nice and warm inside, but they can teach you a lot. Be like the journalist who prefers to talk to a politician's ex-wife rather than to the current wife. MBNA, the credit card company, had senior managers listen in on customer calls for four hours each month, including calls by customers canceling their accounts. Undoubtedly, more learning came about as a result of this exercise than from any polished presentation of research findings by a market research company.[10]

> *Talk to your ex-customers.*

*3) Recruit at least some sales and marketing people and even the new CEO from the ranks of customers.* Many companies already do this. IBM saved itself by hiring a big old customer – Lou Gerstner – as its CEO. Just about everybody inside IBM – everybody in the computer industry, in fact – knew IBM needed to split itself up fast in order to have a chance at survival. Gerstner knew little or nothing about computers and less about the computer industry, but he had been a customer and therefore he knew – didn't think, guess, speculate, estimate, but knew – that IBM's main problem for customers was a lack of cooperation among product and geographic divisions.[11] This was not a problem to be solved by splitting up but by – the opposite – increasing integration among the different parts of the company. Why couldn't anyone in IBM see this? Because, as they say in China, it's hard to see the mountain when you are on the mountain.

The Container Store is a successful chain, growing at about 20 percent a year for some 25 years now, selling boxes and other things that help you get organized. The store probably attracts a very special kind of shoppers, special people who are well organized. The company recruits these people. Employees carry recruiting cards and when they see a customer they think might be a good employee they try to get that customer to apply for a job. Employees get a $500 bonus for a new hire. The policy must be working: Container Store sells about $400 per square foot per year, more than three times the industry average.[12]

> *Recruit from the ranks of customers.*

*4) Let your customers help you manage.* You should ask customers and potential customers to approve or reject your new advertisements, or at least to sit in on meetings you have with your market research and advertising agencies. A brand manager for a leading detergent in Europe told me, "We always get customer feedback before we run any advertisements." But why process your customers' opinions through the filters of your ignorance?

Imagine the advertising agency knows that housewives will approve or reject their advertisements. Will this influence the way they make the advertisements? I think so. They will now try to make advertisements that impress laundry detergent purchasing housewives rather than laundry detergent advertisement purchasing marketing executives.

Let me note here that you should not, however, ask housewives to compare different advertisements for detergent. Show different advertisements to separate groups of housewives. Then compare the groups' responses to questions such as: would you purchase this product? Would you recommend this product to friends? Those questions will not tell you how many people will buy or recommend the product. But the differences in answers across advertisements will suggest which advertisement is the better one.[13]

> *Your customers are the true experts on your customers.*

*5) Be your own customer.* Learn from Dell's customer service disaster. Call your service hotline with a request for help. Undergo the torture you put your customers through. Stay at your own hotel. At some hotels, when I call for ice, after five minutes an attendant knocks on my door and takes away my empty bucket. In five more minutes he comes back with the bucket filled with ice. Nice.

But it takes about two seconds to figure out that it might be more efficient to do what most hotels do and bring me a full bucket of ice and take away my empty one. This way the attendant saves time, the hotel saves money, I get better service. Why have some hotels not figured this out?

I suspect that the hotel manager does not know about ice cube buckets since he does not live in a room in the hotel. He has an apartment in the hotel with a refrigerator. Recently I found a new twist. The attendant came with a bucket of ice and then, to my astonishment, produced a spoon and slowly scooped the ice from his bucket into my bucket.

> *Be your own customer.*

*6) Be your competitor's customer, too.* See how they do things differently and try to figure out why. Here's another scenario about ice. The Shangri-La hotel in Beijing puts ice in your room around 5 pm every day, whether you ask for it or not. Is it more efficient to do it this way? Maybe it costs more. But every 30 minutes or so, the melting ice makes a little crunching sound, reminding the guest that he or she could have a nice ice cold whiskey. Perhaps the hotel discovered it sells more from the mini-bar with this approach.

If you suggest ideas like this to your marketing manager, listen carefully to his or her response. If your marketing manager says he or she doesn't think this will work for your hotel, or whatever your business may be, fire this person. He or she is a danger to your business. This type of marketing manager tries to do your customers' thinking for them. A good marketing manager, a real marketing manager, will respond that trying the idea on two floors of the hotel and calculating the effect after a month or so will cost very little. If the idea proves profitable it can be done on all floors for many years to come and in all hotels managed by the chain.

By the way, remember to fire your fake marketing managers with the best possible letters of recommendation so that your competitors will hire them. Fake marketing managers do a lot of damage by the sin of omission.

Shop with your competitors to more fully take your customers' perspective and to find ideas and try them in your own business. If the idea doesn't work, you don't repeat it. If the idea does work you repeat it year after year across your operations. You have made your money machine that much better.

> *Be your competitor's customer too.*

## Maximization of customer satisfaction is not the objective

Although the marketing philosophy argues we should take the customer's perspective, this does not mean that maximization of customer satisfaction is our goal. Profit maximization is the goal. We take the customer perspective not because we love the customer, but because we want to better catch the customer. We are the fisherman who tries to think like a fish.

A while back there was a debate in *Marketing News* (the newsletter of the American Marketing Association) on whether marketing is about making love (to our customers) or about making war (with our competitors). Some professors said it was the one thing. Other professors said it was the other thing. Still others said it might be both. Actually, you make both love and war with both your customers and your competitors (and suppliers and allies). We are all joined in a game of trying to get maximum output for minimum input.

It is nice of course to talk about loving, win-win relationships with our customers. But win-win is really saying nothing. All exchange relationships are win-win by definition. Even "your money or your life" is an invitation to a win-win relationship. But how much do *you* win and how much do *I* win? That question is ignored by talk of love and win-win. But it is the central question of marketing.

> *Win-win is nice. How much do you win and how much do I win?*

It is not the goal of marketing to maximize customer satisfaction by discovering what customers really want. Dilbert, the famed comic-strip philosopher, offers insight on what customers really want: "What they want is better products for free."[14]

If your customers are truly and deeply satisfied and tell you they would never go to your competitor, not even if you doubled the price, then what do you do? You conclude they are too satisfied so you double the price.

You try to do as follows. Keep the customer sufficiently satisfied so the customer stays with you and tells others to come to you. Any additional satisfaction you balance out by increasing price and your profit.

If you succeed in making the customer completely dependent on you, then maybe you can forget about customer satisfaction altogether. It is even possible that customer satisfaction becomes a negative for you. For a near-monopolist like Microsoft, for example, current sales are the main competitor of future sales. If Microsoft was to satisfy its customers it would reduce sales of upgrades. This explains why new versions of Word contain subtle new ideas to frustrate customers (such as footnotes that randomly insist on spreading themselves out over two or three pages), while popular and even essential features, such as "split screen" and "reveal codes" are taken out.

*Fortune*'s info-tech columnist Stewart Alsop has noted that software you have to use, such as Word or Outlook, is designed to "really drive you crazy,"[15] while optional stuff, like Palm synchronizer or Google, works smoothly. He wonders, "If there's some way the people, Microsoft, who make the frustrating software could learn how to design their programs as though they were optional." The answer, unfortunately, is that the "driving you crazy" features of Microsoft software do not reflect Microsoft's incompetence, but rather its genius.

> *The better your marketing, the less important is customer satisfaction.*

## ✍ POINTS TO REMEMBER

- ☞ The value of a company rests on its customers.
- ☞ It is hard to see what your customers see if you live in a different world.
- ☞ Nobody loves you like you do.
- ☞ Feel your customers' pain.
- ☞ Surround yourself with reality.
- ☞ Talk to your ex-customers.
- ☞ Recruit from the ranks of customers.
- ☞ Your customers are the true experts on your customers.
- ☞ Be your own customer.
- ☞ Be your competitor's customer too.
- ☞ Win-win is nice. How much do you win and how much do I win?
- ☞ The better your marketing, the less important is customer satisfaction.

## Notes

1. Peter Lynch and John Rothchild, *One Up On Wall Street: How To Use What You Already Know To Make Money In The Market*, 2nd rev. edn (Simon & Schuster, 2000).
2. Zesiger S. "Can Cadillac Come Back?" *Fortune* (18 September 2000), pp. 170–177.
3. Keith Regan, "Will PlayStation 3 Be an Online Shopping Tool?" *E-Commerce Times* (24 January 2001); Jan Howells, "Sony to Offer Online Banking via Playstation 2," *vnunet.com* (31 March 2000).
4. Ben Elgin, "Can Anyone Save HP?" *Business Week* (21 February 2005), p. 28.

5. Katrina Brooker, "I Built This Company, I Can Save It," *Fortune* (30 April 2001), p. 94.
6. Googlefight.com offers the opportunity to match different brands or actors, and so on, against one another, based on the respective number of Google hits on "I hate X."
7. Brooker, "I Built This Company."
8. "A Cable Company People Don't Hate," *Business Week* (28 May 2007), p. 73.
9. For a detailed story on the customer service debacle at Dell, see "Dell in the Penalty Box," *Fortune* (18 September 2006), p. 70.
10. Frederick Reichhel and W. Earl Sasser, Jr., "Zero Defections: Quality Comes to Services," *Harvard Business Review* (1990), pp. 105–11.
11. Louis V. Gerstner, *Who Says Elephants Can't Dance?: Leading a Great Enterprise through Dramatic Change*, reprint edn (Collins, 2003).
12. Vicky Powers, "Finding Workers Who Fit," *Business 2.0* (1 November 2004), p. 74.
13. Detailed information on how you can test advertisements before you run them is found in John R. Rossiter and Larry Percy, *Advertising Communications and Promotion Management* (McGraw-Hill, 1997). The book is still very useful and practical today, though admittedly it doesn't have a chapter on interactive digital TV advertising.
14. Scott Adams, *Slapped Together: the Dilbert Business Anthology* (HarperCollins, 2000), p. 137.
15. Stewart Alsop, "When It Comes To My PC, I Can't Love It Or Leave It," *Fortune*, 28 April 2003.

# 4 Do We Know Anything in Marketing?

---

## Key messages to whet your appetite

▶ Knowledge is the best currency
▶ Discover. Test. Improve. Be scientific
▶ Marketing is a game of chance
▶ Manage your odds

---

## Who needs to know anything anyway?

*It is generally accepted that you don't need to know anything to do marketing. To do accounting, law, surgery, plumbing, carpentry, cooking, you need to learn things, perhaps pass an exam and get a license before you are allowed to practice. For marketing there is no exam, no license, nothing to know. Anybody can practice marketing without ever studying marketing.*

*Another generally accepted sentiment is that, in marketing anyway, there are no right or wrong answers. Too many professors, misguided pseudo-sophisticates, actually say exactly that. I think they heard it somewhere in the 1960s or 1970s. Then they wonder why students complain about grades. Professors should know better. Students provide us with plenty of wrong answers. They love to lower prices for example without worrying about competitive responses and without calculating, without being able to calculate, the impact on profitability, or the increase in sales necessary to make up for the lower price. It is true that most of the time there may be several right answers, but that does not mean there are no wrong answers.*

*In this chapter I argue that the "I know nothing and I'm proud of it" approach to marketing is wrong. I give examples of marketing knowledge,*

31

*and I give examples of how such knowledge can be used to improve a firm's marketing results. The great thing about marketing knowledge is that typically we can use it to improve marketing results without increasing cost.*

## Everybody can do marketing

Or at least everybody thinks everybody can do marketing. Engineers or journalists or English majors routinely take on marketing assignments. Hospitals use medical doctors to do marketing. Computer companies like to use computer engineers. Sometimes it works; sometimes it doesn't.

Michael Dukakis used a brilliant law professor from Harvard to run his election campaign. Some 150 different brilliant commercials later his huge (17 points or so) lead had turned into a big defeat by a few simple commercials, endlessly repeated, by Bush I. This sort of thing does not happen in accounting, dentistry, plumbing, engineering or the legal world. Certainly, few marketing professionals hire themselves out as brilliant lawyers.[1]

But everybody is an expert on marketing. For example, how difficult is advertising, really? Show the product, have girls sing, a baby smile, a cute old person boogie, a great headline ("Power"), and that's it. Or shake the camera a lot, MTV-style, some screaming, and, bingo, you have your edgy Gen-X ad. Or make a lame joke with a Buddhist yoga monk and some incomprehensible sentences; your dot.com ad is all done.

> *There are plenty of right answers in marketing, and there are plenty of wrong answers too.*

There actually is much to know in marketing. But many people in marketing and especially in advertising know little or nothing about marketing or advertising. There are many marketing managers who just "play" marketing manager, the way five-year-olds play Mommy and Daddy without knowing it's not really how Mommy and Daddy play. If you are reading this book you are probably not one of them. At the very least you won't be one of them after you finish reading this book.

Like the five-year-olds playing Mommy and Daddy, managers who lack knowledge naturally don't know what they don't know. Therefore, they assume there is nothing to know. Since the outcome of marketing actions – good or bad – can often be ascribed to a variety of causes, it is not too difficult for unknowing marketing managers to hide the truth from themselves and others – that *they don't know what they are doing.*

In contrast, when dentists or accountants make mistakes, when the drill goes through your cheek or the books don't balance, these mistakes are more easily noticed. This ambiguous quality of marketing is most unfortunate because, as we will see, there are indeed wrong answers in marketing.

When a company looks for a new VP of marketing, it is considered unremarkable when that new VP is hired on the basis of his resumé, after interviews with an HR manager who has a degree in Sociology and a CEO who is an engineer. Your PR agency announces, "Company X's new marketing VP has broad experience with a number of leading companies in different industries." Meanwhile the handsome new VP you are so proud of might be a shining example of "when you get run out of town, stay ahead of the crowd and make it look like a parade."

Over the years I have worked with many companies, but only once has a company asked me to test a new marketing manager it was thinking of hiring. Tests are not perfect of course, but nothing in marketing or life is perfect.

> *Find out if that bright new marketing manager you want to hire knows something about marketing.*

Below are a few examples of useful marketing pieces of knowledge. Throughout this book I hope to add to your store of useful knowledge.

## People really, really hate to lose

Prospect theory from economics[2] has found that the risk aversion finance talks so much about is only half the story. The other half is just the other way around: when people face the prospect of loss they display a risk preference hoping to avoid the loss. They seek risk; they are willing to pay for risk. In a well-known example, suppose you are offered the following options:

A: Get $30,000 for sure

B: Get 80 percent chance on $40,000 with 20 percent chance of getting nothing

What do you choose? If you are like most people you will choose A. We know that on average, B is the better choice. The value of option B on average is $32,000. But we don't live our lives on average. Averages are not so interesting when you can choose only once. Most of us are willing to give up some potential gain in order to eliminate risk. This we all know. Thus, on average we get $30,000. We gladly *pay* $2,000 to *avoid* risk.

Now consider the following two options:

A: Lose $30,000 for sure

B: Take 80 percent chance of losing $40,000 with 20 percent chance of losing nothing

Now what do you do? Faced with this choice, the great majority of people prefer B. Thus, on average we lose $32,000. This time around we gladly *pay* $2,000 to *get* risk.

These results are useful for marketers. First, if you want someone to buy from you, especially when you are a new supplier or offer a new product, you are asking that person to take risk. Since people are willing to take risk to avoid loss, do not tell them what they will gain if they accept your offer; *instead, tell them what they will lose if they do not accept your offer.*

Good salespeople for cars or houses love to use this weakness of ours against us. "This is a really nice car for you. But, to tell you the truth, if you don't buy it now you will lose it for sure." It works even better if the salesperson adds, "I didn't tell my boss yet, but I have someone else for this car who'll come back tomorrow to buy it." A shared secret of impending shortage – "Nobody knows this yet" – multiplies persuasive power.[3]

My wife once bought a car and then found out I had to co-sign the loan. Looking at the papers I noticed they had taken her for a ride, adding life insurance on the loan and a maintenance and repair warranty. So I called the dealership and told them I would co-sign provided they take off the insults to our pocketbook. They called her first, and she called me, not too happy: "He said I might lose the car because of you." How many cars are there in America? One hundred million? She didn't lose the car.

> *Tell potential customers what they will lose if they do not buy.*

In addition, customers' loss aversion means we should look for opportunities in our customer relationships to build in elements of loss for customers in case the relationship breaks down. We can offer warehousing space, financing, promotional support, and so forth. The more things like this we offer, the more the customer stands to lose when the relationship is broken. As a result, we can demand more and more from the relationship. In fact, we will demand rewards that exceed the expense of our generosity. Customers might obtain a net gain by breaking the relationship, but they might not. "Might" is the operative word here. Loss aversion biases the customer against walking out on us.

*Loss aversion is stronger than risk aversion.*

## If you want to tempt customers, distract them first

Experiments show that when customers are distracted they tend to go with feelings rather than thoughts. One experiment by Professor Baba Shiv asked two different groups of people to memorize a two-digit number and a seven-digit number, respectively. Then participants in the experiment were asked if they would like a piece of chocolate cake or a fruit salad. Remarkably, 41 percent of the two-digit group wanted chocolate cake compared to 63 percent of the seven-digit group who wanted chocolate cake.[4] It appears that a busy brain can't pay as much attention to what the body ought to eat.

When you wish to appeal to greed, fear, or desire; when you wish for irrational rather than rational decisions, distract the customer. That's why casinos offer you loud clanging, banging noise rather than relaxing piano music. So you can't think.

If you try to sell an extended warranty on a car, appealing to fear, ask how many cars the customer has owned since his first car, make sure you have the radio set to Rush Limbaugh or a rap station instead of easy listening music, introduce the customer to three different people within five minutes (actually, car dealers do that already). Will that work? If you have a real marketing manager she will be curious to try.

By the way, distraction works for the seller because it diminishes the capability of the buyer's brain. Is this manipulation ethical? I imagine that it is not. But Pandora's box, once opened, can't be closed. My duty is to teach you all that might be useful to you. It seems high time though that marketing works as hard to share knowledge with customers as it does to share knowledge with marketing managers. Economics is considered to be for everyone. In contrast, marketing only works for managers. Marketing journals, for example, always insist on a discussion of research implications for managers, but never worry about implications for customers. I am thinking that my next book should be for customers: "How Companies Fool You Every Day."

> *Emotional appeals work better when you distract customers.*

## If you cannot distract them, make them sad

In the movie *The Wedding Crashers*, the main characters join wedding receptions because it's easy to pick up girls there. A repulsive friend, however, reveals that he prefers to go to funerals because they are even better than weddings. Professor Baba Shiv would think so too. When he asked people to recall sad memories, he found that sad memories too led more people to eat chocolate cake rather than fruit salad.[5] Similarly, sad movies relative to comedies lead people to consume more popcorn.[6] Sadness and unhappiness impede conscious, rational decision-making.

Happiness on the other hand has a positive effect. For example, people in a happy mood because they just found a coin in a payphone appear to be more creative as well as thorough in their decision-making.[7] People with happy personalities tend to search for more information, consider information more thoroughly, and make better decisions in business simulations.[8] (Make a note to your HR department to hire happy people.)

> *Sadness too helps reduce rationality of decisions.*

## Send men to women and send women to men

Research shows that men are more likely to get a raise when they ask a boss who is a woman rather than a boss who is a man. The reverse holds true for women who are more likely to get a raise when their boss is a man rather than a woman.[9] Men and women are genetically programmed to compete with their own gender and cooperate with the opposite gender. So when you need a cooperative response from customers, better send a woman to a man, and a man to a woman.

> *Gender wars are a myth.*

# Beautiful women reduce men's ability to (dis)count

Would you like $100 today or $200 one year from now? If you are a man, your answer depends in part on whether you are looking at a beautiful woman. Experiments show that men are more likely to take the $100 today after looking at pictures of beautiful women.[10]

The experimenters' explanation is the Darwinian idea that for men the best reproductive strategy is to take any opportunity that comes along. Put a man in a reproductive mood and his ability to think long term is destroyed.

For women the best reproductive strategy is to think about the long term implications of choosing one man or the other. As a result, feeling sexy or not, or maybe especially when feeling sexy, women worry about roofs that need fixing or about loan payments five years hence.

There has been a longstanding debate about whether sex sells or not. Here is your simple answer: Sex sells the short term to men but un-sells the long term. Sex won't sell life insurance or gardening supplies. Sex sells beer, cigarettes, sports cars, and payday loans. If you want a man to spend money without worrying about being in debt for the next ten years, or dying in a car crash or from cancer, first show him a beautiful woman.

> *Sex sells whiskey. Your uncle sells life insurance.*

# Getting little favors gets you to getting big favors

A company I worked with has a sales force of about 200 people. The company's owner, a practical scientist, always looks for interesting experiments to run. Once he heard about a door-to-door sales company, selling the Rainbow vacuum cleaner, presumably instructing its salespeople to ask for a glass of water at the beginning of the sales presentation. Reportedly, this small request improved the closing percentage. The company owner instructed 30 of his salespeople to ask for a glass of water at the start of their presentation. After a few weeks, he found that sales for the experimental group had increased by about 3 percent. Next, he instructed the group to ask for a soft drink. This request did not help sales at all. This favor was too big to be effective.

Why do little favors lead to big favors? The little favor is an investment in a relationship with you. Since everybody hates to lose an investment, the person who did you the little favor becomes reluctant to break the relationship with you by denying you a bigger favor. Another explanation is that the little favor someone does you makes them think they must like you. Consistency would call for continuing to like you – and do you the big favor.

> *Little favors lead to big favors.*

This man is a very successful business owner. Let us consider in some detail the way his mind works. First, he reads about what other companies are doing. But, of course, a lot of business people do that. Second, he does not think about whether an idea will work or not work for his situation. He thinks about how he can test the idea, how to find out if it will work for him, or if he can make it work. He is a dispassionate scientist in action. Third, he starts thinking and testing as to how he can improve the idea.

There are people who manage and there are people who pretend to manage. Compare the scientific manager and his open-minded experimental approach to the way of a marketing manager who pretends to be a marketing manager and will look at a new idea and tell you, "I don't think this will work for us. Our situation is different. Our customers are different."

> *Discover. Test. Improve. A good marketing manager is an experimental scientist.*

## The professional manager applies knowledge

Marketing education teaches the principles of marketing much better than it teaches application of these principles. Marketing professors often despair at the inability of the educated to apply what they were just educated in, and at our own inability to change this, although we try as best we can. Let me try here, too.

What do you want to accomplish in business? If you are not the CEO of your company already, one thing you want to accomplish is a promotion. So how do you apply the knowledge you just acquired to this challenge?

People really hate to lose. So make sure your boss knows you can be lost if you don't get a promotion. Are you chocolate cake or fruit salad?

Are you a morally challenged underachiever or a reliable producer with good scores on all the required diplomas? If you really don't deserve the promotion, during discussion of possible promotion distract your boss with irrelevancies, plus make her sad by sharing stories of your orphanage upbringing, plus, in case your boss is a man, show a picture of your beautiful younger sister to help him forget about any long-term damage he is doing to the company by promoting you. If you are a man, try to be assigned to a woman boss, and vice versa. Also, ask your boss if you can leave an hour earlier to pick up your mother at the airport. If the boss says "yes," you offer the appropriate "thank you," and then proceed with: "Probably now is not a good time, but I was wondering if we could talk about possibilities for my promotion ... ." Because your boss did you the small favor, he or she will be more inclined to support your promotion.

> *The key to successful marketing is the use of marketing knowledge you have.*

So what is knowledge? Maybe you find yourself thinking about the above recommendations, "This will not always work." Then maybe you are an engineer.

To engineers, all this marketing stuff does not sound like truth or knowledge at all. What bothers them is that these marketing truths are not always true; in fact, they are quite often not true, sometimes even not true most of the time. For disciples of the hard sciences, if something is not always true, it is never true. For engineers, 100 centimeters is always one meter. Thus, when I say, "Women do the grocery shopping," a female engineer might respond, "No, not true; my husband does the grocery shopping."

But in marketing, nothing is always true. In marketing, when we say, "It is true," we mean that it is "true enough" or "true for all practical purposes." By this we mean that *if you believe it and act accordingly, you will be better off than if you don't believe it.*

> *In marketing, "true" means "true enough."*

Thus, if a salesperson can close more deals by first asking for a glass of water, this shows that having done you a small favor, people will *more likely* grant you a bigger favor. The likelihood might have gone from a mere 1 percent to a still small 1.25 percent. That means 99.75 percent of the time, asking for water has no influence on the yes or no decision. But when the likelihood goes from 1 percent to 1.25 percent, this also means you have 25 percent more sales by asking for water.

Doing things right does not guarantee success; it improves the *probability* of success. In this way, marketing is like gambling. We never know what card the dealer will turn over.

Can you make money gambling? Guaranteed? Long term? Absolutely! Be the casino. When people gamble, the casino gambles too. There is just one small difference. The casino wins 51 percent of the time; everybody else wins 49 percent of the time. As a result, 100 percent of the time, sooner or later, the casino wins 100 percent of the money. Marketing is like gambling; it's not risky when the odds are in your favor. What are the right answers in marketing? The right answers in marketing are the answers that improve the probability of you winning.

> *Marketing is like gambling. If the odds are in your favor gambling is not risky.*

## ✍ POINTS TO REMEMBER

☞ There are plenty of right answers in marketing, and there are plenty of wrong answers too.

☞ Find out if that bright new marketing manager you want to hire knows something about marketing.

☞ Tell potential customers what they will lose if they do not buy.

☞ Loss aversion is stronger than risk aversion.

☞ Emotional appeals work better when you distract customers.

☞ Sadness too helps reduce rationality of decisions.

☞ Gender wars are a myth.

☞ Sex sells whiskey. Your uncle sells life insurance.

☞ Little favors lead to big favors.

☞ Discover. Test. Improve. A good marketing manager is an experimental scientist.

☞ The key to successful marketing is the use of marketing knowledge you have.

☞ In marketing, "true" means "true enough."

☞ Marketing is like gambling. If the odds are in your favor gambling is not risky.

# Notes

1. The problem with Susan Estrich, the Harvard law professor in charge of Dukakis's presidential campaign, was not merely that she did not know about effective advertising. She was intuitively opposed to effective advertising as reflected in her comment in 2004 on Fox News (http://www.foxnews.com/story/0,2933,117830,00.html): "What's the line between figuring out which ad works and figuring out, 'How do I manipulate this particular voter through a combination of words and images in order to convince him to believe something he may not really believe?'" She has a valid point. When money drives public debate, will the best ideas survive or will the best advertised ideas survive? But such fine moral sensitivity did not help Dukakis win. Antipathy toward effective advertising is not unique to leftish law professors. Inside any advertising agency you will find plenty of "creatives" who shudder at the thought that their art might persuade somebody to buy something.

2. Daniel Kahneman and Amos Tversky, *Choices, Values, and Frames* (Cambridge University Press, 2000). For several decades now it seems that all interesting new thinking in marketing has been generated outside marketing by economists, psychologists, sociologists, and so on.

3. For more about persuasion, you should read Robert Cialdini's fascinating book, *Influence: Science and Practice* (Allyn and Bacon, 2001), not just to learn how to be successful in persuasion yourself, but also to learn how to avoid unwanted persuasion by others.

4. The experiment was done by Baba Shiv, Professor of Marketing at Stanford University, reported in his article, "Heart and Mind in Conflict: Interplay of Affect and Cognition in Consumer Decision Making," *Journal of Consumer Research*, Vol. 26 (December 1999), pp. 278–82. In a similar vein, also note his article, "Influence of Consumer Distractions on the Effectiveness of Food Sampling Programs," *Journal of Marketing Research*, Vol. 42 (May 2005), pp. 157–68.

5. Baba Shiv, "Let Us Eat and Drink, For Tomorrow We Shall Die: Effects of Mortality Salience and Self-Esteem on Self-Regulation in Consumer Choice," *Journal of Consumer Research*, Vol. 32 (June 2005), pp 65–75.

6. Brian Wansink, *Mindless Eating – Why We Eat More Than We Think* (Bantam, 2006). This book describes a whole range of hidden factors that cause people to eat more than they should. Darwinism predicts that the food marketing practices that will lead you to eat more rather than eat less will survive in the market place.

7. Higgins Qualls and Couger, "The Role of Emotions in Employee Creativity," *Journal of Creative Behavior*, Vol. 26 (1992), pp. 119–29;

A.M. Isen and B Means, "The Influence of Positive Affect on Decision-making Strategy," *Social Cognition*, Vol. 2 (1983), pp. 18–31; A.M. Isen and R.A. Baron, "Positive Affect as a Factor in Organizational Behavior," *Organizational Behavior*, Vol. 13 (1991), pp. 1–53.

8. B. Staw and S. Barsade, "Affect and Managerial Performance: A Test of the Sadder-but-wiser vs. Happier-and-smarter Hypotheses," *Administrative Science Quarterly*, Vol. 38 (1993), pp. 304–31.

9. Martin Georg Kocher, Ronald Bosman, Matthias Sutter and Frans van Winden, "Experimental Evidence of the Importance of Gender Pairing in Bargaining," presented to the Royal Economic Society Conference, 2004.

10. Margo Wilson and Martin Daly, "Do Pretty Women Inspire Men to Discount the Future?," *Biology Letters supplement 4*, Vol. 271 (7 May 2004), pp. 177–79.

# 5 Marketing's Job

## Key messages to whet your appetite

▶ Define customer quality
▶ Classify customers
▶ Manage your customer portfolio

## Great customers

*It is marketing's job to create great customers. Companies need to define and measure customer quality, and link marketing managers' rewards to maintaining and improving customer quality. As products are becoming more and more commoditized, competitive advantage increasingly will rest on differences in customer quality.*

*Earlier I argued that R&D is part of marketing's job. R&D of markets and marketing is necessary to discover how to find and keep great customers. Later I will argue that getting better prices than our competitors is part of marketing's job. Getting better prices is a result of getting great customers. Better prices in turn offer the margins that allow us to invest to keep our great customers. Everything we do in marketing links back or should link back to finding and keeping great customers. Our customers define who we are.*

## Marketing's job is to produce great customers

It is not enough just to sell our products. It matters greatly to whom we sell. The factory's job is to produce great products. Marketing's job is to produce great customers.

We compare companies' products, size, sales growth, assets, debts, employee relations, production costs, and so on. But we rarely compare their customers:

What is the average income, age, and education level of the Wal-Mart versus K-Mart versus Target versus Sears shoppers?

What is the average growth rate of companies buying from one supplier versus those buying from another supplier?

Is the average age of the Wal-Mart shopper increasing? Is the average age of the Cadillac buyer decreasing?

If you need to judge the value and future prospects of a company, you should look for data on customer quality. I am convinced that data on customer quality and changes in customer quality better predict a company's present and future prospects than financial data.

But most companies today still lack even a definition of customer quality. Companies should classify and rank customers much in the way that many HR departments classify and rank employees. Then marketing's job is to sell our products to identified great customers, to constantly work to improve the quality of our customer portfolio. We know people by the friends they keep. In the same way we know companies by the customers they keep.

> *We know companies by the customers they keep.*

The implications of defining marketing's job as that of creating great customers are not necessarily intuitive. The benefit of a focus on building customer quality is that it guides us to taking actions in the short run that will pay off greatly also in the long run. Let me illustrate.

When demand for raw materials such as copper soared in China, a large producer told its Chinese distributor: "We don't need your sales force and we don't need your marketing because there is more demand than we can satisfy." The producer therefore demanded a huge cut in the commissions paid to the distributor. The distributor was my EMBA student and so he asked me what I thought about his situation.

In order to design a proper response to the producer's demand, the first question to consider is: does the producer have a good point? Is marketing less necessary in a seller's market? When demand exceeds supply, should sales and distribution turn into mere order-taking? Whenever I raise this question in a seminar, managers agree that marketing is less necessary during periods where demand exceeds supply.

> *Common sense tells us marketing is less necessary when demand exceeds supply.*

Suppose you get paid $30 per hour in January, but $15 per hour in February. Would you wait until February to put in many hours because it is more necessary then? Obviously you wouldn't. You would like to put in more hours in January and take off in February. Marketing is the same. Marketing is less necessary when demand is strong. But at the same time the payoff for marketing effort is higher when demand is strong. Let me show you why.

Manufacturing produces products. Marketing produces customers. Higher-quality products offer competitive advantage, so do higher-quality customers. In markets for commodities the products are in principle the same. Copper is copper. But definitely the customers are not the same. Some customers are:

▶ more financially sound,
▶ likelier to survive in the longer run,
▶ growing faster than their industry,
▶ more stable in demand,
▶ better referenced,
▶ less expensive to serve,
▶ and so on.

Two companies, with identical products, but different in the quality of their customers can show very different results. What is the value of market share in the fast-growing Chinese consumer markets when compared to market share in the declining Japanese consumer markets? What is the value of a customer who buys from you continuously, compared to a customer who switches in and out, always looking for a better bargain? If your customers are all 70 years old and my customers are 20 years old, does not my future look brighter than your future? How happy is BMW when Tom Cruise decides to buy a BMW?

So do we need marketing when demand exceeds supply? Absolutely! When demand exceeds supply we are handed a great opportunity to enhance the quality of our customer portfolio, to increase the quality and value of our most important asset determining the true value of all our other assets and of our total company. In the case of the commodities distributor, let us take this opportunity now to identify the companies that are most competitive in their industry, that are most financially sound, that are growing most rapidly, that cost least to serve, that are the least price-sensitive, and so on. Let us now spend money to approach these companies, let us now offer them great service and attention. Let's go talk to them while they are glad to hear from us. Let us do these things while our competitors are cutting back on marketing and reverting to nasty monopoly habits.

> *Common sense is wrong: marketing pays off best when demand exceeds supply.*

Consider the impact of such a strategy. Imagine two companies, A and B, selling a pure commodity. A saves money by eliminating marketing. A simply sells its output to anyone willing to pay its price. In contrast, B romances the best customers of A, visits them even as A's salespeople have stopped visiting because A's salespeople have been let go, encourages these best customers of A to contact B for any additional supplies they might need, and hopefully signs some of them up for long-term contracts. B also reduces or stops delivery to its less attractive customers. Those less attractive customers, formerly of B, now are forced to go to A. Over time B will exchange its least desirable customers for A's most desirable customers. Company A might notice that its costs start creeping up (less attractive customers cost more to serve). But A's marketing managers won't do a study to show how A's absence of marketing is increasing total costs for the company in areas such as accounts receivable collection, inventory expenses, transportation expenses, and so on. If A's marketing managers were clued in enough to study the damage B was inflicting on them, they wouldn't have let B inflict the damage in the first place.

In the short run, B's profitability will improve relative to A's profitability. That is one bonus for B. In the longer run, inevitably, additional companies will enter this seller's market and turn it into a buyer's market again. Perhaps the new companies steal 20 percent of B's customers. Fortunately for B, perhaps its great customers are growing at 20 percent a year on average. Even when 20 percent of its customers leave, B still produces and sells at 100 percent capacity. Let A, with its less attractive customers, more price-sensitive customers, financially weaker, with less growth, also lose 20 percent of customers. Then A needs to find new customers. A needs to find new customers just when this is most difficult, when the market has become a buyer's market. A approaches companies when companies have no longer any particular need to listen to them. A will need to offer discounts, to sell at prices less than the market average, in order to get customers to switch. A will end up with less attractive customers paying lower prices.

Company B captured its customers in a seller's market, in January so to speak. Company A has to capture its customers in a buyer's market, in February. It is hardly surprising that the result will be that company B will spend less effort and money while also finishing up with better customers.

> *When the going gets good, the smart get going.*

One could say that in the competition between A and B, company B has a better strategy than company A. But it is more accurate to say that company B is the company with strategy, while A is the company without strategy. Company A loses the game, not because it does not play the game well. Company A loses the game because it does not play at all, because it does not even know that during a seller's market the game is on for better customers.

I am not surprised that a raw materials producer should think marketing unnecessary during times of raw material shortages. It is quite easy to forget about marketing in an industry where products are very much the same or even identical. It seems intuitive that marketing cannot help much in an industry where there is no opportunity to differentiate the product from competitors. But this intuition is wrong. Even when product differentiation is not possible, customer differentiation is always possible. When product differentiation is not possible, customer differentiation becomes especially important. Maybe your product is the same as my product, but I will still win when my customers are better than your customers.

Some managers say, "All that counts in our industry is price, nothing else." When they say "nothing else," they are thinking about products and they may be right about that, but they forget about customers. When my customers pay more quickly, switch supplier less often, grow more, cost less to serve … I can win price competition because my customer quality gives me a cost advantage.

> *When your products cannot give you advantage, your customers can give you advantage.*

Beware of handing out bonuses only based on sales performance. Measure also the quality of the customers brought in by your marketing department. When you have accounts receivable problems, don't just look at the finance department for answers, don't just tighten standards and payment terms. Look also at your marketing department. Maybe they have found a way to make their life easier by identifying customers other companies are too smart to serve. Companies should measure lifetime customer value and reward marketing and sales, not merely for bringing in customers, but for bringing in valuable customers.

IBM once offered generous buy-out packages to employees willing to leave the company voluntarily. IBM's HR department was shocked when it found that A-rated employees, the best 20 percent of employees, happily signed up for the buy-out package. When your best employees decide to leave your company, you can have no doubt left that you are in serious trouble.

Marketing can learn from HR. When we implement new pricing schemes, new service policies, new positioning strategies, new products, what is the effect on our best customers? When old customers leave and new customers join, who are these new and old customers? Many HR departments work hard to rank and classify employees. Many marketing departments can learn from these HR departments and should work just as hard to rank and classify customers. The next two chapters will expand on these ideas, discussing management of markets and new ways of market segmentation.

---

*Learn from HR: classify and rank your customers.*

---

### ✍  POINTS TO REMEMBER

- ☛ We know companies by the customers they keep.
- ☛ Common sense tells us marketing is less necessary when demand exceeds supply.
- ☛ Common sense is wrong: marketing pays off best when demand exceeds supply.
- ☛ When the going gets good, the smart get going.
- ☛ When your products cannot give you advantage, your customers can give you advantage.
- ☛ Learn from HR: classify and rank your customers.

# 6 Managing Your Markets

```
┌─────────────────────────────────────────────────────────────┐
│                                                               │
│  Key messages to whet your appetite                           │
│                                                               │
│  ▶ Know your market well                                      │
│  ▶ Believe what you see, not what you believe                 │
│  ▶ Manage your segment environment                            │
│  ▶ Fight the wounded and dying                                │
│                                                               │
└─────────────────────────────────────────────────────────────┘
```

## Your markets

*Who are your customers? Where are your customers? How about your competitors' customers? In this chapter we first emphasize that an important part of marketing's R&D job is to ensure that we know and understand both our own customers and our competitors' customers.*

*Next we lay out eight market characteristics that determine whether a market is healthy for our company, or not. The first five characteristics follow Michael Porter's famous five forces framework. Here we examine the proactive management of these forces at the market-segment level rather than viewing them as uncontrollable factors determined by a company's industry environment. The additional three characteristics concern issues of right size, growth and profitability, and accessibility.*

## How well do you know your market?

To know your market, you should not just know your own customers; you should also know your competitors' customers. For example, many companies measure customer satisfaction. But I ask companies something else too: "Do you measure your competitor's customers' satisfaction?"

Ninety percent of the companies I ask tell me they don't. Well, I then say, in that case you think you know how well you perform on customer satisfaction, that most critical dimension of performance, the one dimension of performance that predicts future performance, but in fact you don't.[1]

> *If you don't know your competitors' customers, you don't know your own customers.*

It is certainly not easy to know even your own customers. Cherished assumptions about your customers may be completely wrong. Campbell's soup, in its early years, provides a nice example of wrong assumptions. The *Saturday Evening Post*, a magazine at that time for middle-class Americans, was trying to convince Campbell's to put advertisements in the magazine. Campbell's demurred, arguing that higher-class Americans were the customers for its fine soups, not the lower-brow readers of the *Saturday Evening Post*.

So Charles Parlin,[2] ad salesman for the *Post*, went through the trouble of collecting garbage bags from a working-class neighborhood in Philadelphia and fishing out all the Campbell's soup cans he could find. Then he returned to Campbell's with the results. Now impressed, Campbell's did some more research. It found that the upper classes did not buy canned soup. The upper classes had servants, and the convenience of canned soup had no value to them. Because Campbell's did not know its customers, it did not know its competitors (the servants), and thus it did not know itself.

> *Know the market. Know yourself. Test your assumptions.*

The Campbell's story was a long time ago. But the more things change, the more they stay the same. Consider the story of Friendster, the original social networking site before Facebook and MySpace. Hottest new Internet site and start-up in 2003, it was dead by 2005.

What happened? Here is one thing. Their director of engineering, Chris Lunt, wondered why traffic always spiked at 2 am. So he looked at the data about customers and discovered more than half of Friendster's traffic came from Southeast Asia, courtesy, as it turned out, of one of the very earliest members of the website being from the Philippines, making half of its eyeballs worthless to its advertisers. That little discovery halved the value of Friendster.[3]

How come the CEO and marketing managers of Friendster didn't know about this until the director of engineering came to tell them? What were they busy doing every day? The fact that the engineering director had to discover the customers tells us all we need to know. We know top management of Friendster wasn't spending any time at all at the website. If they didn't even know on which side of the world the majority of their customers lived, did they know age, race, gender, education, hobbies, and so on? Wonder why Friendster got killed so quickly by MySpace and Facebook? Now you know.

> *Make sure your CEO and marketing managers know who your customers are.*

Today's cash register data help to know our customers a little better since they tell us what else our customers buy. Thom Blischok, business sciences chief at NCR in 1992, doing a market-basket analysis for client Osco Drugs, uncovered the famous correlation between beer and diapers purchases. Beer and diapers intuitively don't go together until someone tells us they do. Babies use diapers. Mothers put diapers on the baby (don't get excited. I'm not saying they should, just that they do). Fathers go buy the diapers and some beer while mother takes care of the baby.

Another correlation uncovered by Blischok is that of cold medicine and juice sales. For marketers of cold medicine, or juice, or juice blenders, this can be very interesting information. My Walgreen's pharmacy doesn't sell juice blenders but perhaps they should: stock them right next to the cold medicine.[4]

Stores maybe cannot keep detailed track of the tens of thousands of items they sell, but a manufacturer definitely should spend time in the store and visually inspect who, how, when, with what, and so on, a product is sold. Data-mining has become popular with the advent of scanner data and computers. What stopped marketing managers before from simply going to the store and looking in the shopping baskets of people buying their product? What's stopping you now?

> *Don't just read about your customer. Look at him and her.*

I remember working on marketing ideas for a new refrigerated fresh pasta brand. I went to the store to educate myself on the category and found that several packages of this company had gone from square box to something more like a football. The product inside was producing some sort of gas. Over the next few weeks, despite my having informed the company of what I thought might be a PR disaster, footballs kept showing up. At the same time I kept getting reassurances that the problem didn't really exist. I never understood that. Obviously not many people working for the company visited stores where the product was sold, or not sold.

A more general example of a widespread and often false assumption among marketing managers about customers is that those who are the first to buy new products, the so-called innovators, are younger and better educated than later buyers. This assumption is wrong. The first customers who buy a new product are people who use the product a lot and/ or who can afford an initially high price. For example, for a new brand of heavy-duty detergent, the typical innovator is a middle-aged housewife with a large family, not a yuppie from Manhattan. The first mobile phones went to older business managers, not the younger ones.

> *Test your assumptions. Measure your market.*

But measurement of our market is not enough. We must also believe in, and act on, the results of our measurements. Note, for example, the battle between Nokia and Motorola in cellular phones. Many consumers consider Nokia to be the more fashionable brand. This was an important advantage when the market became younger and more female, driven more by consumers than by business.

Occupation by Nokia of the fashion position in the cellular phone market has been quite an achievement for an old-time rubber boot-making firm from Finland. Why was Nokia the first to make the phone a fashion item? Did Nokia possess superior consumer research skills? I doubt it. Motorola certainly has equal capabilities.

Instead, in my opinion, Nokia's advantage was the early, high level of penetration of the cellular phone market in the Scandinavian countries. The future happened sooner in Finland than in Illinois. Nokia's managers saw the future sooner with their own eyes in their own homes and neighborhoods, listening to their own wives and sons and daughters buying phones. Motorola may have known that women and young people were becoming major customers, especially in Northern Europe, but this was not yet the obvious case in Illinois. Measurement of the market does not work when we discount the result based on our preconceived notions.

*When you don't believe the data, maybe they told you something you didn't know.*

## Managing Michael Porter's five forces

Since we can identify or invent any number of market segments, we need to decide which segments are worth pursuing. Which segments are attractive? What are the criteria?

Harvard Business School professor Michael Porter lists five forces that determine industry profitability.[5] These forces were originally identified in industrial organization, a branch of economics worried about how companies use market power to stifle competition. The five evil forces threatening to stifle competition are of course five good forces from the point of view of strategic management or marketing, ensuring profitability.

You have probably heard about these five forces before. But I want to make an important point here. The five forces are generally presented as industry conditions to which we must adapt. At the industry level, the five forces are indeed largely uncontrollable.

But at the level of market segments – the level where we make our money – the forces are quite controllable or avoidable. It's marketing's job to manage these five forces, to build a great market segment for itself, filled with great customers.

*Manage the five forces affecting the profitability of your industry segment.*

The five forces:
*1) Entry barriers.* How easy and attractive is it for competitors to get into your market? The easier it is for competitors to enter, the less money you will make. This is one of the reasons restaurants are a tough and risky business.[6] Yes, I know there are many long-time successful restaurants. I love to go to Antoine's in New Orleans, a restaurant open since 1840, so sure of itself that it locked one of its dining rooms, the Japanese Room, after Pearl Harbor and didn't reopen it again until the 1980s. (You and I might have changed the room's name, but that's why we're not Antoine's.)

Yet for every Antoine's, there are many more restaurants that don't make it. The intensity of competition does not leave much margin for error. Even Antoine's may not survive the impact of Katrina.

Cheap rental housing, antique shops, restaurants, independent gas stations, all face the problem that it is easy to enter. So everybody enters, few make money, and even fewer make good money.

Do you possess or can you create significant entry barriers? This is a critically important issue to consider when evaluating the attractiveness of a market. What can you do to create barriers in your market, or market segment, where none existed before?

Maybe you can have your industry association talk to your government about better consumer protection. A great thing is always when government creates new regulations while grandfathering in your operation. Any new restrictions on an industry tend to be good for the incumbents. The elimination of cigarette advertising on TV, for example, certainly didn't hurt the existing players in the industry.[7] The big players in the cigarette industry know this very well. For example, when Thailand prohibited cigarette advertising on television, Philip Morris and friends, who were trying to build market share against local competitors, got the US government to put pressure on the Thai government to rescind this presumably protectionist measure.

> *Don't be where others can join you.*

*2) Rivalry.* In some industries leading competitors are very polite to one another. The cereal industry is a good example – although they would beg to differ. Advertising and limited shelf-space provide the entry barriers; politeness ensures the huge margins on carton boxes filled with mostly air. In contrast, Coca-Cola and Pepsi do not just compete – they are bitter rivals for world domination. When the embargo against Vietnam was dropped, the Saigon hotel where both Coca-Cola and Pepsi managers were staying instituted separate dining hours for managers of the two companies to put an end to the throwing of cans. In another example, Rick Bronson, delivery truck driver for Coca-Cola, was fired for drinking a Pepsi on the job.[8]

With that kind of rivalry, it seems not a good idea to enter the cola market, especially in the U.S. Richard Branson, the famed British entrepreneur, nevertheless entered with Virgin Cola. This was a bad idea. Coca-Cola and Pepsi killed Virgin Cola without trying. Virgin Cola was a mouse entering the ring to join two fighting elephants destroying everything around them. Virgin Cola flopped pretty much immediately in the United States, despite a promising start. Today the company has retreated mostly into creative drink niches. It wasn't for lack of trying or lack of creativity. The introduction was much energized by creative and irreverent Virgin/ Branson marketing stunts. But some battles are just too big. Branson was well aware of the danger. He considered it a worthwhile gamble only because the cost of failure would be low, with cola being so incredibly cheap to produce that in his opinion it should be hard to lose a lot of money selling it.[9]

> *Don't look for fights, especially not with someone bigger than you.*

*3) Substitute products.* Competitors may hurt you, but substitutes can kill you. Industry insiders, unfortunately, may be the last ones to recognize that their industry will soon be gone. Hanny Magnetics in Hong Kong proudly announced world leadership in floppy disks after a major acquisition in 1995, just as data storage and transfer went to CDs and the Internet. Coleco, in the 1980s, developed a tape recorder for computers that was ten times faster than regular tape recorders, and you needed to buy their special tapes too, so you can see the potential. Too bad disk drives became cheaper and built in, not exactly an unforeseeable development. Coleco could, of course, lower its prices, but it is hard to keep lowering your price – especially once you get below zero. You can't fight an incoming tide, and at some point you have to ask yourself, "Are we history?"[10]

New technologies typically start out inferior to the old technology and are most easily shrugged off by those who have the deepest understanding of an industry. Compare the car to the horse, for example. A horse does not run out of gas, rarely breaks down, does not get stuck in the mud, can go almost anywhere, while the car can go almost nowhere. If you have too much to drink or fall asleep, your horse is still smart enough to bring you home, provided you don't fall off. The more of an expert you would have been on horses and cars, the better you could have explained why the car would never be more than a fad, fun for rich people to drive in a limited range around their house in good weather. All the horse needed, you might have said, is modification to incorporate the latest technological advances, like maybe attach a plastic roof to the saddle.

But the horse is gone, and so is the typewriter, the corner grocery store, the tape recorder, the pager, the fax (well, not yet), centralized oil- or gas-fired electrical power plants (another 50 years experts say, but experts also said we would run out of oil by the mid-1980s). There is nothing inherently wrong with not running out too soon on your old market. Except that it is very easy to go down a slippery slope, to start subsidizing the past at the expense of the future.

> *Once you are history, do go gentle into that good night.*

*4) Power of buyers.* When buyers are powerful, suppliers suffer. Companies generally are smart enough to avoid becoming too dependent on a single customer, but accidents happen. When customers merge and acquire, suddenly you may find yourself caught in a vise where you cannot afford to walk away from a customer. Remember that when your merging customers talk about realizing efficiencies from the merger, it is just a nice way of saying they plan to put your money into their pocket.

But mistakes are made too. Several companies entering China in the early days failed to realize the implications of a command economy. With their Western eyes they saw a market comprising numerous enterprises in the steel or cigarette industry, but all those enterprises belonged to one ministry. In reality there was only one buyer. Invoices from a deal with one company were shared among all companies. A low introductory price for one company would become the starting point for new negotiations with other companies in the same industry. A purchase manager for any other company, copy of invoice at hand, would not – indeed could not – agree to a higher price. It is hard to make money if you have only one buyer.

> *When buyers can put more of your money into their pockets, they will.*

*5) Power of suppliers.* Maybe you start a very successful restaurant in a really nice building. Your landlord comes to eat in your restaurant sometimes and sees how well you do. You are very happy. You landlord is even happier than you are because your money will soon be his money. What can you do? Close your successful restaurant? Ray Kroc, who started McDonald's, was a fanatic on this point. To remain in control of his destiny, Kroc always insisted on owning the land beneath his restaurants. As a result, for a long time, until the policy was relaxed to allow 20-year lease arrangements, there were few McDonald's restaurants in places like Manhattan.[11] Remember this: you cannot make money if you cannot control the bargaining power of suppliers.[12]

Sometimes the supplier that kills you is inside. Note the constant bankruptcies of airlines in the U.S. Why does it happen? One of the big reasons is the stranglehold pilots in particular have over the airline. When the pilot does not show up, a $20 million-plus airplane sits idle. Until airlines solve this problem, the industry will never prosper. One idea has been to offer part ownership of the airlines to employees, but the flaw in that scheme is obvious. Pilots (and machinists) prefer to take all the profits rather than part of the profits. Professional sports teams have similar problems when top players can make or break a team. We make a distinction between suppliers, employees, and customers, but sometimes the distinction is mostly a legal fiction.

> *When suppliers can put more of your money into their pockets, they will.*

## Searching for the worst industry

The common interpretation of Michael Porter's five forces model is that firms searching for new opportunity should identify markets where the five forces are favorable. Such an interpretation leads to the paradoxical advice that you should try to enter industries that are difficult or impossible to enter.

I never gave this any thought until I won an assignment from a large food company to identify attractive markets in China's dairy industry for entry. Following some significant amount of data collection and analysis, and long discussions, the inescapable conclusion was that we should look for just the opposite of the traditional ideal market as suggested by the five forces model. We should look for the worst market, where the incumbents are interested only in looking for exits and golden parachutes. Entry will be easy, will be encouraged by suppliers, customers, local governments, even incumbents. Now you just have to make sure that you manage the five forces properly in whatever corner of the industry you decide to set up shop.

My thinking about entering new industries therefore is that it doesn't matter so much which industry you go into (provided you don't enter an industry that is on the verge of disappearing, say, typewriters in 1980). What truly matters is what you do in your industry once you are there. All else equal, though, it is much better to enter a "bad" industry rather than a "good" industry.

> *Find a battlefield, filled with wounded and dying competitors.*

Some of the most successful companies in the world (Dell, Southwest Airlines, Wal-Mart) started out in industries that were commoditized (PCs), and/or at the mercy of powerful suppliers both internally and externally (airlines), or fiercely competitive (discount retailing), or dominated by well-established, big companies with strong brand names (all of the above).

Michael Porter's five forces model predicts that companies will find it difficult to make money in industries suffering from unfavorable conditions. From a marketing perspective, however, we are not interested in industries. Companies do not compete in industries. Companies compete in segments. Mercedes Benz and Volkswagen are in the same industry but not in the same segment.

> *Companies don't compete in industries; they compete in segments.*

So when a company wishes to know if a particular industry should be entered, my question is: what will you do in that industry once you get there? What new segment will you build? What new mountain of your own will you stand on? Where is your Blue Ocean?[13]

Michael Dell made himself king of a special new segment: people incapable of fixing their own computer, but who do not wish to be without a computer for as much as several weeks. This niche turned into a pretty big segment. The first computer buyers were computer lovers. The next 99 percent were computer users rather than lovers.

Wal-Mart, aside from its important innovations in the logistics of large-scale retailing, also found success by creating and serving a new segment: selling at discount prices to the middle class. The existing discount stores, such as industry leader K-Mart, sold at discount prices to the lower class. I have seen no figures, but I have a sense that K-Mart is still seen as low class, while Wal-Mart is seen as middle class.

Southwest Airlines was perhaps the most radical new-segment creator of all: they are less an airline than a bus company. They do not use tickets and boarding cards or seat assignments. You want a window seat? Hurry up and you might get one. You want to eat on the plane? Bring your own food. Travel agents want 10 percent of the ticket price? Southwest Airlines gave them nothing.

So what will you do when you get to your new industry? You don't have to be better, richer, stronger, or smarter than the current players. But you do have to be different.

> *Don't be better. Be different. Build your own mountain.*

## Three additional characteristics

*6) Right size.* The market or market segment should be big enough to satisfy your ambition, but not so big that you shall never be more than a small fish in a big pond. Define your market segment so it fits your size. Expand your definition, or multiply them, as you expand.

In his book *Jack: Straight From the Gut*,[14] Jack Welch makes an interesting point on defining your market right. Welch and GE are famous for the "be number one or two, or fix, close or sell" approach to business. Less famously, Welch had his mind changed on the long-term wisdom of this approach.

GE managers had taken a class at the U.S. Army War College in Carlisle, Pennsylvania. In that class, an army colonel argued that the number one or two philosophy leads managers to define their markets narrowly to have market leadership. Welch writes:

> For nearly 15 years I had been hammering away on the need to be #1 or 2 in every market. Now this class was telling me that one of my most fundamental ideas was holding us back. ... I took their idea ... [asking the business units] to redefine all our current markets so that no business would have more than a 10 percent market share.

Sales growth at GE doubled over the next five years. You can see why Welch richly deserves his title as one of the greatest managers of the 20th century. He heard something new from a class of managers who conveyed the thinking of an army colonel who was denying well-established Welch wisdom. Because what he heard made a lot of sense to him, he took action without apology or delay. This shows how Welch brought to GE a culture where managers were willing to tell him he was wrong, and he brought that rare mind that did not ask, "What the hell does an army colonel know about business and GE that I don't know?" He looked at the idea. He didn't feel threatened. He got excited.

> *If you can't be proven wrong any more you need to retire.*

7) *Growth and profitability.* Growth and profitability are good things. As mentioned before, when your customers are growing and making money, you won't be hurting either.

8) *Accessibility.* Some marketing textbooks warn against defining a market as, for example, "optimistic people." Since there are no magazines aimed at optimistic people, and you cannot buy Nielsen data on optimistic people, there is no way to economically access a market defined as "optimistic people." But marketing textbooks are wrong about this issue. It is important to access your market economically, but this does not mean you need to define your market in terms of the variables by which the media describe its audiences. Rather than identifying how old your customers are and then buying time in media reaching that age group, you should simply go to your customers and potential customers (whatever their age and so forth). Ask *them* which TV programs they watch and which magazines and newspapers they read. (There is more about this in my discussion of media selection.)

---

### ✍ POINTS TO REMEMBER

- ☞ If you don't know your competitors' customers, you don't know your own customers.
- ☞ Know the market. Know yourself. Test your assumptions.
- ☞ Make sure your CEO and marketing managers know who your customers are.

- ☞ **Don't just read about your customer. Look at him and her.**
- ☞ **Test your assumptions. Measure your market.**
- ☞ **When you don't believe the data, maybe they told you something you didn't know.**
- ☞ **Manage the five forces affecting the profitability of your industry segment.**
- ☞ **Don't be where others can join you.**
- ☞ **Don't look for fights, especially not with someone bigger than you.**
- ☞ **Once you are history, do go gentle into that good night.**
- ☞ **When buyers can put more of your money into their pockets, they will.**
- ☞ **When suppliers can put more of your money into their pockets, they will.**
- ☞ **Find a battlefield filled with wounded and dying competitors.**
- ☞ **Companies don't compete in industries; they compete in segments.**
- ☞ **Don't be better. Be different. Build your own mountain.**
- ☞ **If you can't be proven wrong any more you need to retire.**

## Notes

1. For studies on the relationship between customer satisfaction and performance, see the recent articles: Neil A. Morgan and Lopo L. Rego, "The Value of Different Customer Satisfaction and Loyalty Metrics in Predicting Business Performance," *Marketing Science*, 25(5) (2006), pp. 426–39; Neil A. Morgan, Eugene W. Anderson, and Vikas Mittal, "Understanding Firms' Customer Satisfaction Information Usage," *Journal of Marketing*, 69(3) (2005), pp. 131–51.
2. Charles Coolidge Parlin went on to organize a commercial research department for Curtis Publishing, the publisher of the *Saturday Evening Post*. Today he is considered to be a father of modern market research. Louis E. Boone and David L. Kurtz, *Contemporary Marketing 2006*, 12th edn (South-Western College, 2005).
3. Max Chafkin, "How to Kill a Great Idea," *Inc.* (June 2007), pp. 84–91.
4. *Todd Wasserman, Gerry Khermouch, and Jeff Green,* "Mining Everyone's Business," *Brandweek,* Vol. 41 (2000), p. 32.

5. Michael Porter, *Competitive Strategy* (Free Press, 2004).
6. About 25–30 percent of new restaurants don't survive the first year of business. About 60 percent are gone within three years of opening. H.G. Parsa, John T. Self, David Njite, and Tiffany King, "Why Restaurants Fail?" *Cornell Hotel and Restaurant Administration Quarterly*, 46(3) (2005), pp. 304–22.
7. Cigarette advertising on TV is not entirely eliminated. Antismoking advertisements by tobacco companies are allowed. Those ads surprisingly increase teenagers' willingness to start smoking even though the ads explain to young people that smoking is only for adults. Melanie Wakefield, Yvonne Terry-McElrath, Sherry Emery, Henry Saffer, Frank J. Chaloupka, Glen Szczypka, Brian Flay, Patrick M. O'Malley, and Lloyd D. Johnston, "Effect of Televised, Tobacco Company Funded Smoking Prevention Advertising on Youth Smoking-Related Beliefs, Intentions, and Behavior," *American Journal of Public Health*, 96(12) (2006), pp. 2154–60.
8. Suzanne Presto, "The Cola Wars Get Personal – Coke Employee Fired for Drinking Pepsi on the Job," *cnnmoney.com*, 16 June 2003.
9. www.virgindrinks.com
10. For a detailed description of this early and unique computer, which came integrated with a printer, see http://www.vintage-computer.com/adam.shtml
11. John. F. Love, *McDonald's: Behind The Arches* (Bantam, 1995).
12. Tim Harford, in his excellent book, *The Undercover Economist* (Oxford University Press, 2005), reports that the fantastic margins of selling coffee for two or three or more dollars per cup are largely captured by the owners of prime real estate locations.
13. W. Chan Kim and R.A. Mauborgne, *Blue Ocean Strategy* (Harvard Business School Press, 2005), is your tool belt for thinking about new segments.
14. Jack Welch, John A. Byrne, and Mike Barnicle, *Jack: Straight From the Gut – What I've Learned Leading a Great Company and Great People*, (Warner Books, 2005). A very useful and interesting book with many great examples. It is not about "Jack." Fulfilling the title's promise, it's about what he has learned.

# 7 New Thoughts on Market Segmentation

## Key messages to whet your appetite

▶ Success comes from where you choose to sit
▶ Define your way to leadership
▶ Let your needs drive segmentation
▶ Dare to walk away

## Where you go sit today decides your tomorrow

*This chapter discusses the key decision we make in marketing: our choice of customers. I show new ways of discovering, segmenting, defining, and qualifying markets and market segments. Earlier I argued that marketing's job is to create great customers. Here I apply this idea to the question of segmentation. In particular, I suggest that we should decide first who should be our customers in order for us to prosper tomorrow. Then we figure out what those customers want, how they are different from other customers, and how we can capture and keep those customers.*

*Further, I introduce a method of segmentation from the advertising literature based on the relationship between a company and its (potential) customers. We also discuss market leadership, market segment invention, and the need to focus also on exiting old segments.*

## Drive your market

Standard approaches to segmentation collect data on customer characteristics by which we might divvy up a market. For consumer markets we might collect data on age, education, income, geographic location, psychographics, or product benefits sought. For industrial markets we might collect data on size, location, and industry, and so on. Statistical techniques such as factor analysis and clustering can then crunch those data to divide a heterogeneous customer population into more homogeneous segments.

There is nothing particularly wrong with this approach, but I have another suggestion. In consumer markets, first determine which consumers are the most attractive, lead the way, are fastest growing, and the least sensitive to price. Next, measure and quantify their demographics and psychographics. Then find out what you need to do to make those consumers happy and set out to make them happy.

Similarly, if you are an industrial marketer, first identify the companies that are potential customers. Next classify these companies based on sales growth and profitability. Then, classify and describe the more attractive companies and determine what it would take to make those companies happy. Then make them happy.

Companies talk a lot about being market-driven organizations. But this is very yesterday. If you want to be cutting edge, you should talk about being a market-driving organization. Looking first for the customers you could love – customers who are growing in size or numbers and who are not too price-sensitive and who fit who you are and can be – then figuring out how to make them love you, creating new segments based on your vision of your company's future, is what I mean by a market-driving organization.

The job of marketing is not to identify what customers want and then give it to them. The job is to identify first who are the "great customers" we must have in order to be more successful over the next five or ten years, then identify what those customers want and give it to them.

An example in China is found with Zhongkeda village in Shanghai, a development of 700 villas built in conjunction with the new graduate school of University of Science and Technology China. The company in charge of the development, Zenisun, had studied the nature of successful neighborhoods around the world, particularly neighborhoods and towns co-existing with famous universities. It decided that the quality and value of a neighborhood is determined by the level of education of its people.

In Shanghai, interviews conducted with people shopping for villas confirmed this idea. Respondents commented that "I would very much like to live next to Zhiyi Fan the soccer player, but I would prefer to live next to a scientist."

Having made the decision to attract educated people, the company examined what high-income, educated customers wanted: an entrance with Roman statues and pillars, or just rocks and trees? Larger distances between houses with higher prices per square meter of house, or smaller distances between houses with lower prices per square meter of house? Based on these interviews the design of the village and the houses was then skewed toward the preferences of educated customers.

*Who do you need to be your customer?*

Another example of finding customers we need in order to be successful in the future is the U.S. car market. Baby boomers are getting old now. First, they ensured the success of the Volkswagen Beetle and Toyota, and so on. Then they drove their children around in ever-bigger SUVs. Now they want ... what? Here are obvious suggestions: make cars that are easier to get in and out of. Knobs and handles should not aggravate the pain of arthritis. Flat tires should not strand customers unable to take off the lug nuts. Anything written should be made easy to read. A convenient place to put one's glasses for driving would be nice too. I doubt this will happen. Old people aren't invited to help design cars. But it would be good for sales.

*Better products need features that attract better customers.*

## Segmentation by relationship

The advertising literature suggests another interesting alternative to traditional segmentation approaches. According to John Rossiter and Larry Percy,[1] authors of *Advertising Communications and Promotion Management*, companies should start out by dividing the market into five broad categories on the basis of the existing relationship between brand and customer, as follows:

1. Loyal customers who use only our brand.
2. Favorable switchers who use our brand and competitors' brands.
3. Unfavorable switchers who use different brands, but not our brand.
4. Loyal customers who are loyal to a competitor's brand.
5. Non-users.

The proportions of customers across the different categories naturally varies across different industries. For example, among smokers and beer drinkers we find very high proportions of loyal customers. Among buyers of cereals we typically find switchers. Non-users will be a huge group in some cases – for instance, many people never purchase cognac, a motor bike, or a hat.

The usefulness of this scheme is that it reminds you to use different marketing approaches for these distinct groups. You should not tell your loyal customers or your brand switchers (or ex-customers) to "try it, you'll like it." And you should not tell customers loyal to another brand or brands that "we are not just for weekends any more."

*If you wish to move a customer, start from where he stands.*

## Market leadership and market segmentation

A significant and long-lasting body of research under the heading of the Profit Impact of Market Share (PIMS) confirms what common sense already tells us: market leaders have all the fun,[2] provided they are doing business in stable and growing markets.[3]

Therefore, if you are small but you still want to have fun, you must define your market segment sufficiently narrowly so you can lead it. You can define your market segment more narrowly by focusing on women instead of men and women – or on young women, or young educated women, or young educated black women, or young educated black women in New York City, or Manhattan. You can also define your market more narrowly according to media. You can advertise in both *Business Week* and *Fortune*, or just in *Business Week*, or in the East Coast issues of *Business Week*, or the New York issues of *Business Week*.

The secret to being a market leader and having all the fun is quite simple: you must have the courage to go for 100 percent of 10 percent of the market rather than 10 percent of 100 percent of the market. Be big somewhere rather than small everywhere.

*Be big somewhere rather than small everywhere.*

Playing this way, a smaller player will have one significant advantage over a much bigger player. Smaller players can choose which 10 percent of the market they will concentrate on. They can take the cream of the market, pursuing the faster-growing segments, the more ignored segments, the more prosperous segments. The larger player may then get stuck in the least attractive part of the market. This may have happened to GM. In the passenger car market, it is left mostly with customers nobody has bothered to steal – older, in the middle of the country, in the middle of the middle class. Size and market leadership are two decidedly different things. GM managers bravely wearing pins saying "29" (signifying company-wide commitment to maintaining 29 percent market share for GM) are still learning this uncomfortable truth.

> *When you become a big fish in a small pond, choose a nice pond.*

## Inventing new segments

The surest way to become market leader in your segment is to invent a new segment. You need to do R&D. When I say R&D, you know I'm talking about R&D of markets and marketing.

Chrysler did not invent the minivan. Volkswagen did. Chrysler invented the soccer mom market for minivans. Miller did not invent low-cal beer. Miller invented the yuppie market for light beer. IBM/Microsoft did not invent the personal computer. IBM/Microsoft invented the adult and office market for personal computers. Dell never invented a better computer. Dell invented a better way to sell and service computers.

Segmentation is a creative process. Segments exist when we find a way to create them. Why don't we have men's and women's toothpastes when other body care products have been successfully segmented by gender? Because no one has figured out yet how to do it. When we speak about invention and innovation and R&D, we should turn our minds and creative energies also to the invention of new markets and market segments.

Possibilities for segment invention are near infinite. For example, look at the vitamins market. What segments can we think of? Children, seniors, babies, men, women, pregnant women, women on a diet, body builders, truck drivers who need to stay awake, large families, people suffering from a cold, smokers, shift workers, travelers, people during winter, jet-lagged travelers, pets, cats, dogs, puppy dogs, old dogs, birds, hospitals, prisons, nursing homes, cereal manufacturers, soft drink makers, bread makers, cosmetics companies, convenience stores, pet stores, bars...

The above segments are just the obvious ones. A company in China, Goldpartner, found much success by advertising that its multivitamin/minerals pill did not contain those minerals which are already plentiful in the standard Chinese diet. Their segment is those consumers who worry that a pill that has everything might have too much of something. Make sure you don't keep your marketing department too busy to do R&D. Insist they set aside time to think about innovation.

> *R&D on new products is good, but start with R&D on new markets.*

## Saying goodbye

We always look for segments to sell to. We might also look for segments not to sell to! I worked with a chemical company facing a painful future in one market because many new plants were under construction. Since transportation costs were quite high, I suggested they draw circles around the sites of future competitive plants and drop customers within such circles now, rather than wait to be dropped by these customers later when it would be much more difficult to replace these customers. Alternatively, they could raise the price now on these customers to compensate for the near certain loss of business in the near future. Simply put, if you soon will lose a market or market segment because of new technology or new competitive entry or other causes, you should focus on exiting with the largest amount of profit.

Particularly if you are in a situation where oversupply looms, it is a good idea to abandon your slow-growth customers sooner, rather than later, and replace them with fast-growth customers. Remember our earlier discussion of the Chinese distributor of commodities.

But marketing is adamantly opposed to abandoning old customers, probably because abandoning old customers makes marketing's job more difficult in the short run. Sure there may be a big payoff in three to five years. But by that time the marketing manager will have another job. So if you as a marketing manager abandon old customers, you make your job more difficult for yourself, and you make your job easier for the next person to hold your job. In the interest of your company's future, should you make yourself look worse while making the next person look better? Maybe you should, but I doubt you will.

Marketing is inclined to see its job as getting the product sold and satisfying customers. A proactive approach to market selection for future success at current expense finds few supporters in the marketing department. Companies should be careful not to let the marketing managers relax at the expense of their company's future. Build a customer base on which you can build a future.

A manager once objected, "But if you abandon all your old customers, how do you know you can find enough new customers?" Gradualism in thinking does not come naturally to all people. There is no need or suggestion to replace all old customers. But suppose a company stops supplying its "10 percent worst" customers (you don't have to kick them out, you can just raise prices on them and if they don't leave, well, maybe they are no longer your worst customers). I believe that if most companies find only one average-to-good new customer for every two "10 percent worst" customers abandoned, they will have done themselves a big favor. GE's fashion of dropping the 10 percent worst managers seems to be spreading. Maybe dropping your 10 percent worst customers is not a bad idea either.

A lot of companies will tell you that they make 80 percent of their profits on 20 percent of their customers. Implicitly, they may thereby assume that they make 20 percent of their profits on the remaining 80 percent of customers. But it is entirely possible that there is a bottom 10 percent yielding a net loss. Unfortunately, notwithstanding the slogans about customer orientation, most companies know their profits by product, not by customer.

> *Losing good customers is bad, but dropping bad customers is good.*

A very different motivation against exiting is the inclination to fight courageously in the face of adversity. This is a bad idea. Business is just business, and the ethic of "no retreat and no surrender" is nice and heroic but inappropriate. You might posture to your competitors that you will never leave, never give up. But while you try to fool them, don't fool yourself.

Still a yellow-bellied chicken attitude is not so easy when we like to live up to an image of the fearless conquering warrior hero – or heroine. *Fortune* just loves to start any profile of an inevitably hard-charging CEO with an anecdote on how the CEO in his spare time thunders around on his Harley Davidson or some other such macho pursuit.

In marketing we should not be warriors, we should be gamblers – making sure that the odds are in our favor, and we should be ready to fold, walk away, or run, when the game turns against us.

*War is hell.*

---

 **POINTS TO REMEMBER**

☞ **Who do you need to be your customer?**
☞ **Better products need features that attract better customers.**
☞ **If you wish to move a customer, start from where he stands.**
☞ **Be big somewhere rather than small everywhere.**
☞ **When you become a big fish in a small pond, choose a nice pond.**
☞ **R&D on new products is good, but start with R&D on new markets.**
☞ **Losing good customers is bad, but dropping bad customers is good.**
☞ **War is hell.**

---

## Notes

1. If you have responsibility for advertising and promotion this is somewhat painful but nonetheless a must-read, a thoroughly practical and very complete reference for all questions you might face: John Rossiter and Larry Percy, *Advertising Communications and Promotion Management* (McGraw-Hill/Irwin, 1997).
2. Robert D. Buzzell, Bradley T. Gale, and Ralph G.M. Sultan, "Market Share – A Key to Profitability," *Harvard Business Review* (1 January 1975), pp. 98–105.

3. When markets decline or when markets change radically, larger firms have less ability to retreat to a niche or to pursue markets based on new technologies, even as physical, technical, and human resource assets are tied up with old technology. For a concise overview on this issue see "Giants Need to Dust Off Their Dancing Shoes to Stay on Top," by Simon London, *Financial Times* (14 December 2005). For ideas for dealing with this issue see *Leading the Revolution* by Gary Hamel (Harvard Business School Press, 2001).

# 8    Lost Customers

**Key messages to whet your appetite**

▶ Cut your defection rate in half
▶ Nail your back door shut
▶ Romance your ex-customers
▶ Build stickiness

## A hole in your bucket

*Imagine in your company you tape all business meetings and conversations for a whole year. What percentage of those millions of words would be about lost customers? How much discussion is there in your company on which customers left? Why they left? Where they went? What you can do to get them back?*

*If you go to work and the computer is missing from your desk I think you will call company security. Somebody will come to your office, question when you last saw your computer, whether you locked your door, whether perhaps the thief came through the window. An e-mail would go out to all employees warning them to be careful, perhaps locking their offices also for lunch. Maybe the company will chain the computers to the desks.*

*But what happens when a customer leaves? He bought his car from your dealership, but for his next car he went somewhere else. He ate dinner four times at your restaurant and he has not returned again. This customer loss is far more serious in terms of damage than a mere computer.*

*So who is calling security? Who is calling the police? Where is the e-mail to all employees? If the computer thief sends an e-mail talking about his theft, what made him do it, and how he did it; we would analyze that e-mail in great depth. A lost customer might send an angry letter too when he leaves. Does that letter get the same attention as the thief's letter?*

*Companies stand at their front door and call out to potential customers: "Come on in, great party here!" Meanwhile our competitors stand at our back door and say: "Keep walking, there is an even greater party over there." Before you go stand at the front door, nail the back door shut.*

## A key segment: lost customers

While we may want to fire customers, at least some customers, we don't want customers to fire us. Any market can be divided into potential customers, current customers, and ex-customers. Among these three segments, ex-customers should receive primary attention. When we know who our ex-customers are, and we understand what made them leave, and we discover what makes them come back, we stand a better chance of keeping current customers and finding new customers.

Companies nonetheless spend but little time talking about ex-customers and spend even less time trying to win them back. Many companies have no idea who their lost customers are or how many customers they lose. In a discussion about brand loyalty I asked a TV manufacturer once what percentage of people who have bought their TV also buy the next TV from them. They didn't know. I had to ask: why do we talk about brand loyalty when we don't even measure it? In contrast, a cell-phone manufacturer I worked with does a survey every three months to determine who buys its phones, who switched to another brand, and which other brand they switched to.

> *Find out who your ex-customers are, and where they are now.*

One reason companies don't spend time with ex-customers is that it is unpleasant to interact with people who don't love you any more. Another reason is that the costs and benefits of losing or not losing customers are not intuitive and, in my experience, are vastly underestimated. When I talk to managers about ways to reduce annual customer defection rates from, say, 10 percent to 5 percent, they are polite and interested, but they are not very excited. Five percent just doesn't sound like much of a difference.

But the difference between losing 10 percent or 5 percent is keeping customers for five years or ten years. Put simply, if you cut customer defection rates in half, then customer life span doubles and future profit on customers doubles.[1] Profit should more than double, in fact, because in most industries customers become more profitable over time for reasons such as declining costs of service, fewer accounts receivable problems, reduced price sensitivity, and so on. Cutting customer defection rates in half doubles the value of your company because it doubles the value of your customers.

> *Cut your customer defection rate in half and you will have doubled the value of your company.*

When customers leave we may think they were not very good customers anyway. The customers who leave might be the ones who were always complaining, reducing their purchases, and asking for price discounts. The unpleasantness of the divorce blinds you to the fact that here was a customer who once was a great customer, a customer who loved you so much they tried to get you to improve before they finally decided to say goodbye forever.

Most customers don't bother to say goodbye. They do like we do when we eat a disappointing meal at a restaurant. When the proud owner of the restaurant stops by our table to ask if we liked the meal, we say: "Oh yes, it was delicious." On our way out we say to one another: "Remind me to never go here again."

In many industries it takes special effort to find out who is leaving, and whether these 'leavers' are our best or worst customers. But in some industries it is easy. For example, every roadside restaurant knows that everybody knows that truckers know where the good deals are. When truckers leave this is visible immediately to the restaurant and to all non-trucker customers of the restaurant. That's why some roadside restaurants have window booths that are "Reserved for professional drivers only." They want to make sure they keep their truckers.

But we are all roadside restaurants. The best customers in any industry are also the customers who are best informed, and the most sensitive with respect to differences in quality and value, and who have the most influence on other customers, and who have the most incentive to leave when they are not satisfied.

If you visit a city once, it is not worth the trouble to find the best hotel. If you visit a city ten or 20 times a year, you can justify a greater effort to search for the best place to stay.

The best customers therefore are the first to leave. They are your canary in the coalmine. The process whereby their leaving also runs off your other customers and reduces the inflow of new customers is generally more subtle and invisible than the simple case of a roadside restaurant with no trucks parked out front. But that process is real nonetheless.

Ex-customers are like nuclear waste in the marketplace. They don't evaporate. They are still out there. Customers know customers, and they talk about their suppliers with one another: "Yeah, we used to buy from X for years but now we don't buy anything from them any more. We buy everything from Y." No amount of lovely advertisements can overcome such comments. You too are a roadside restaurant. Who are your truckers? How much do they love you?

> *Find out who your best customers are. Make sure they have reason to love you.*

Doubling the value of the company is nice and hopefully you are excited. But it's not the biggest benefit from cutting your customer defection rate in half. Here is the biggest benefit. If you stop losing customers you can invest more to get new customers. If you earn $500 rather than $250 on a typical customer, you can spend more on acquiring new customers. If you spend more than your competitors on acquiring new customers, you will get both the best new customers and the most new customers.

MBNA offers a very impressive demonstration of the impact of losing fewer customers. In 1982 MBNA decided to make losing fewer customers a priority. A special swat team was assigned the job of winning back ex-customers. Analyses were conducted to determine what made customers become ex-customers and policies and strategies were changed accordingly. MBNA decided that to fill a bucket of water, first there should be no holes in the bucket. When MBNA started its "keeping customers is the first priority" strategy, the company was #38 in the industry. Eight years later MBNA was number 4.[2] Losing fewer customers is the fastest way to higher sales, higher prices, and lower costs.[3]

Once I was coming out of a theater in New Orleans when I was stopped by two nice women, who wanted to know if I wanted a free souvenir T-shirt. Well, I said I wouldn't mind, of course. In that case, they informed me, all I had to do was fill out an application for the MBNA credit card. MBNA can afford to spend more to go hunt for better customers because they have figured out now not to lose the customers they catch.

> *Learn from MBNA.*

# Keeping customers

How ex are your ex-customers anyway? Poor service, poor products, and high prices will drive customers away. But don't forget about simple inertia. Many customers stop doing business with us for no particular reason. They forget us. In an experiment by a jewelry store, customers were called with a simple "thank you for being our customer" message and with a "thank you for being our customer, we have a special discount for you" message. Sales increases were especially high for customers who had not purchased for a long time. Also, the message without the special offer generated more additional sales.[4] It appears that at least some portion of ex-customers need no more than a simple reminder of our existence.

> *Remind your customers of your existence.*

It is interesting that the simple reminder phone call worked better than the offer of a special discount. If you must pay customers to come back to you after they have experienced your product and service, you have a problem. The "thank you, here is 20 percent discount if you return" phone call raises suspicions that the store is a bit too desperate. Offering special discounts to customers to try a product makes sense; we pay them for the cost and risk of trying something new. Offering discounts for people to repeat purchase makes less sense.

Many so-called loyalty programs are sales promotion tools offering bribes in situations where loyalty does not exist. They are not really loyalty programs at all. Sales promotions such as frequent flyer miles and credit card points, and so on, have their place, but it is easy to go down the slippery slope of forgetting what makes your best customers come back, replacing the work it takes to create loyalty with bribery.

You may recall the war between long distance companies MCI and AT&T. Whenever a customer switched its long distance supplier, the companies would call the customer to offer special incentives, like a $75 check, to come back. I had a friend who made a science of switching back and forth just to get the incentives. Bribery is just another form of price competition, and price competition creates neither love nor wealth.

Your very best customers should be more interested in the quality of your product and service than in bribes.

Professor Don Schultz made this argument, asking: "Do business class and first class frequent flyers really look forward to flying more for free?

Or are they more interested in everything else the airline does for (and to) them?"[5] Loyalty schemes may be popular with marketing managers for the very reason we should be careful in using them: loyalty schemes can take the place of marketing managers really doing their job.

> *Don't let your loyalty programs replace loyalty.*

We can organize our business in ways that will make our customer relationships more sticky. People, for example, are more likely to change their spouse than to change their bank. When we open a bank account we set up electronic payments, get a credit card, get a mortgage, and develop a personal relationship with the bank. It takes a lot of work and a bit of emotional pain to switch banks.

It may pay companies accordingly to tie additional offerings to their main offering, not only to increase sales, but also to increase the cost and complexity to the customer of leaving. Telecommunications companies offer bundles that can include Internet service, cable service, mobile phone service, and landline service. You have to be a really angry customer to go through the hassle of changing all those services all at the same time.

> *Design sticky customer relationship.*

---

✍ **POINTS TO REMEMBER**

☞ Find out who your ex-customers are, and where they are now.
☞ Cut your customer defection rate in half and you will have doubled the value of your company.
☞ Find out who are your best customers.
☞ Make sure they have reason to love you.
☞ Learn from MBNA.
☞ Remind your customers of your existence.
☞ Don't let your loyalty programs replace loyalty.
☞ Design sticky customer relationship.

# Notes

1. Frederick Reichheld and W. Earl Sasser, Jr., "Zero Defections: Quality Comes to Services," *Harvard Business Review* (1990), pp. 105–11.
2. *Ibid.*
3. Frederick Reichheld has been the driving force behind the idea that better service benefits the supplier as much if not more than the customer. A must-read is his most recent book, *The Ultimate Question: Driving Good Profits and True Growth* (Harvard Business School Publishing, 2006).
4. This experiment is reported in, "A Test of Positive Reinforcement of Customers," by J. Ronald Carey, Steven H. Clicque, Barbara A. Leighton, and Frank Milton, *Journal of Marketing*, 40(4) (October 1976), pp. 98–100.
5. Don Schultz, "Foster Loyalty the Old-fashioned Way: Earn It," *Marketing News* (4 June 2001), p. 5.

# 9  You Don't Know Good Advertising

> **Key messages to whet your appetite**
>
> ▶ Don't talk to yourself
> ▶ You can't judge your ad
> ▶ Your agency can't judge your ad
> ▶ Experiments are insurance

## You and I: we don't know good advertising

*When we see our company, we primarily see our boss, our subordinates, our office, the headquarters building, the factories, fellow managers, the products. In sharp contrast, the customer primarily sees the advertisements, the promotions, the salespeople, the packaging, and the product. Additionally our marketing managers and advertising agencies spend their working lives thinking, maybe for weeks, sometimes months, about an advertisement. Customers meanwhile spend but five or ten seconds looking at that advertisement.*

*Because managers and customers see and live in different realities, it is very difficult for managers to create or judge effective promotions for customers. If nothing else, remember this about advertising: you can't judge your own advertisements.*

## Avoid the managerial perspective

Many advertisements take a "managerial perspective." For example, a magazine advertisement by Canadian insurance company Royal & SunAlliance announces, "You have our attention, no matter which corner office you are in." No other information appears in the ad, just this headline on a blue background showing two vague office buildings. The advertisement assumes that customers already know the company and its products and will be grateful for the company's attention. The ad offers no clue what the company does for a living. Real estate? Corporate travel? Customers who don't know this company will have to decipher some nearly illegible, small print in the corner.

Royal & SunAlliance knows what Royal & SunAlliance does, but when I use this ad as an example in my seminars, at most 10 percent[1] of middle and senior managers can connect the company with its business.

> *Tell your customers what you do for a living.*

An advertising campaign by Emerson Electric is another example. This is a great company but, like so many technical companies, it is much better at making technical things than advertising.

The advertisements show strong-looking men and women proudly gazing at you under a big headline that reads "Power," with some little story in the lower right corner in tiny white letters. (All advertising agencies love to put text in little hard-to-read white letters; they do this to show their unique creativity.) Power? Emerson Electric does not produce or sell power – electric or otherwise.

How exciting or informative are these advertisements to potential customers? Have they tested these advertisements with their customers? I think not. Or maybe, as happens in many cases, the testing was done by their advertising agency through a focus group, using a biased investigator and the wrong methodology.

Much research has been done on headlines and advertisement effectiveness. Based on research results from Gallup and Starch readership studies, we know that five times as many people read the headline than read the copy. If your brand name is not in the headline, most people who see your ad will not know it is your ad. When you put your headline in quotes, recall goes up by 28 percent. Headlines that don't say what the product is or what it will do for you score about 20 percent less in recall.[2]

So what do you think? Is "Power" a good headline? When you are thinking about your headline and your advertisement, think about your customer and what would make him or her want to read your ad.

> *Talk to your customer.*

## An exercise

Let us do a little exercise. Fred Smith Adhesives ran the same advertisement in the same magazine, but with two different headlines. Half the copies of the magazine showed the ad with the one headline, and the other half showed the same ad with the other headline. The two headlines were as follows:

1. Fred Smith Adhesives: Products You Can Stick With
2. Fred Smith Adhesives: A Company That Sticks With You [3]

Which headline worked better? Which headline takes the customer perspective? Which headline takes the company perspective? Ask yourself: what does the customer want? What does the company want?

Readers of the magazine were called and asked whether they remembered seeing an advertisement for Fred Smith Adhesives. The advertisement with the first headline was recalled by 16 percent; the second headline scored 4 percent. Obviously, the headline is very important, and your headline should address what your customer wants rather than your own hopes and dreams.

> *Don't talk to yourself.*

## The wrong way to decide on your advertising

From *Fortune*, 8 November 1999, "The $20 Million Company ... And Its $40 Million Ad Campaign," we can learn the wrong way to decide:

> Peter Badad[4] is sitting on the edge of his seat in a conference room at the ad agency Young & Rubicam in San Francisco. Badad is the brand manager for Covad, a Silicon Valley company that sells high-speed access to the Internet, and he is about to review Y&R's final cuts of two television commercials. They will be the centerpiece of a $40 million, yearlong, coast-to-coast marketing campaign designed to trumpet little-known Covad as a broadband leader. A lot is at stake,

especially when you consider that Covad's sales for the past 12 months totaled just over $20 million, or half its marketing budget. But what really has Badad anxious right now is one of the spots. At last viewing, the supposedly humorous piece had fallen flat. And there are just two weeks left until the campaign launch.

The lights dim, and the commercial's director cues the first spot. The scene: a yoga studio bathed in warm, late-afternoon sun. An instructor oozing New Age smarminess gently tells his students to "assume the jasmine-blossom position, and I'll print the moon charts." But there's a problem: Dialing up the Internet on his standard-issue 56K modem to download the moon charts, the yoga man can't connect. Stung with the same frustration that has bedeviled virtually every Net surfer at some point, he loses his Zenlike cool, screams, and smacks his PC. Title cards pop up that read, in succession, FASTER ACCESS and ALWAYS ON, ending with the just revamped Covad logo. Badad's tension evaporates. "Wow, I'm really impressed," he says with a laugh. Unlike the earlier version, the spot is funny and the message clear. The Y&R creative team smiles with satisfaction.

Do you see anything wrong with this picture? If you don't, it is a good thing you are reading this book. Frankly, this sort of thing makes me bang my head against the wall with frustration. Though I should know better, I still find it unbelievable that companies will ignore so fundamentally everything that is known about advertising. Pity the poor investor who will be poor indeed – whose money is so cavalierly, so ignorantly thrown out the window.

I have suggested to a friend of mine who runs a stock fund that he should start a short-selling fund concentrating on companies that run ridiculously dumb advertising campaigns. Not because advertising is the only factor contributing to a company's success, but because advertising is one of the few opportunities we have to gauge directly the capabilities of senior managers. My friend would have made a bundle in this case.[5]

So what is wrong with the picture? Who is least able to evaluate the effectiveness of any ad? The answer is simple: (1) the people inside the company for whom the ad is made, and (2) the people who made the ad. So who are the only people involved in Covad's ad evaluation? Exactly.

> *The advertiser and its advertising agency are least able to judge their advertisement; they know too much.*

The best person to judge your ad is the prospective customer! This, I would think, is neither deep theory nor complicated; it is the most common of common sense. Before spending $40 million, twice the company's previous year sales – essentially betting the whole company – might it not have been a good idea to run these ads by some prospective customers? Before spending $40 million, Covad should have spent $50,000 or $100,000 running the campaign on one or two news programs in two or three cities, then called around to find people who watched the program to ask a few simple questions: "Did you watch the program. Do you remember any advertisements about accessing the Internet more rapidly? Have you ever heard of Covad? Do you know what Covad sells? If you are interested in Covad's product, do you know how to get Covad?" I used to feel a bit embarrassed sometimes about taking consulting fees for seemingly simple advice. But some simple advice could have saved Covad a lot of money here.

> *The best person to judge your ad is the prospective customer.*

*Fortune*, normally on the ball, drops it in this case. The writer is obviously enthralled with the Internet-ness, new economy-ness of it all ...

> Indeed, a campaign as sweeping [sweeping does seem the right word for blowing the whole company on an untested ad] as Covad's usually needs 14 months; Covad is rolling it out in 90 days. Money and speed, however, do not guarantee a bold, fresh strategy. Conscious of that, Covad CEO Robert Knowling [CEOs are public figures, no point in inventing a name for them] insists they are not going to spend $40 million experimenting.

So not experimenting guarantees a bold, fresh strategy? All the ad time is wasted on a yoga instructor who gets upset because the Internet is slow. A yoga instructor ad that looks like every other Internet ad guarantees a bold, fresh strategy?

Covad and its CEO did spend $40 million experimenting. Unfortunately, they spent it on one experiment, on the basis of the judgment of one man sitting on the edge of his seat, surrounded by the creators of the ad eagerly anticipating his smile. Covad could have spent, say, $100,000 and three weeks, to find out if the $40 million was going to be well spent, and then gone ahead and spent the big money. Why the big hurry anyway? What was the big difference if the main campaign started out at the beginning or the end of October 1999? Money burning a hole in your pocket, Mr. Knowling? Goodbye Covad.

If you don't want to learn by experimenting, you will learn through experience. Learning from experience has an undeservedly good reputation. A smart business avoids learning from experience.

Anne Mulcahy, who led the miraculous turnaround of Xerox, once was asked: "But surely you learned a lot from your experiences?" She responded: "We learned the hard way. It's not a good way to learn. We almost went out of business, we destroyed a lot of market value, we let down a lot of customers, we laid off a lot of employees."[6]

> *Experiments are cheap insurance against learning from experience.*

## ✍ POINTS TO REMEMBER

- ☞ Tell your customers what you do for a living.
- ☞ Talk to your customer.
- ☞ Don't talk to yourself.
- ☞ The advertiser and its advertising agency are least able to judge their advertisement; they know too much.
- ☞ The best person to judge your ad is the prospective customer.
- ☞ Experiments are cheap insurance against learning from experience.

## Notes

1. Exercise/Question: suppose Royal & SunAlliance proves me wrong and shows surveys indicating that at least 80 percent of middle and senior managers know them and their business; even then would I really be wrong?
2. These numbers and more can be found in *Ogilvy on Advertising*, a very popular bestseller written by David Ogilvy (Random House, 1985). The book is also a lot of fun to read. Also recommended is *Tested Advertising Methods*, by John Caples (previous vice-president of BBDO) and Fred Hahn (Prentice Hall, 1998).
3. This example is from *Which Ad Pulled Best?*, by Philip Ward Burton and Scott C. Purvis (NTC Business Books). They have published a

series of editions with pairs of different advertisements for similar or identical products. Each edition is a gold mine of valuable information, provided you have access to the instructor's manual. Only professors can get those, so you'll have to ask your favorite professor. Burton and Purvis should sell the book together with the manual.

4. I changed the name because I'm a nice guy.
5. By the time this $40 million campaign was over, the stock price was down by some 90 percent and the Board of Directors had ousted the CEO.
6. John Battelle, "Turning the Page," *Business 2.0* (July 2005), pp. 98–100.

# 10 What Makes a Good Advertisement?

**Key messages to whet your appetite**

▶ Know the FCB model
▶ Know your selling situation
▶ Learn the rules to break them

## Rules

*In advertising there are many rules to be followed to make advertisements successful. There are nonetheless many people in the advertising industry who don't want to know the rules. They believe rules kill creativity. Actually, the opposite is true. Rules demand greater creativity. To write a poem that rhymes demands more creativity and effort than to write one that does not rhyme. (I am aware that modern poetry must not rhyme. This book actually is a poem.)*

*Professor Armstrong of Wharton University asks: "The question for you is whether you think cumulative knowledge from experts, typical practice, and research can add to your current knowledge."[1] That's a good question. If you think other people over the years, through trial and error, might have learned something that might be useful to you, then this chapter is for you. If you haven't the time to read this chapter because you are busy inventing this round whatchamacallit, don't worry about skipping this chapter. A lack of knowledge about advertising is not going to stop anyone from becoming a great success in the industry.*

## The FCB grid

Back to Covad and Fortune magazine's puff piece...

> [Badad and Worsead] pitched to grandma when they worked together
> at Procter & Gamble, hawking Puffs and Charmin. Believe it or not,
> selling broadband is a lot like selling toilet paper: The marketing chal-
> lenge is to strike the right tone and instill a unique "personality" in a
> product that's pretty much the same no matter who offers it.

"Believe it or not?" Believe it not! Selling broadband is completely different from selling toilet paper. People already know toilet paper. Most know
how to use toilet paper. They have experience with different brands; there is
nothing new or exciting about the product. I suspect Covad's managers sold
broadband the way they sold toilet paper because that is what they knew
how to do. Give a baby a hammer and everything needs hammering.

Everything that could possibly be different is different. Isn't it obvious that the selling approach, including the advertising approach, also
should be different? It is obvious and there is a well-known framework
in advertising discussed in just about any basic advertising textbook: the
so-called FCB grid, created originally by Richard Vaughn at the Foote,
Cone & Belding advertising agency.[2] This grid is based on the common-
sense idea that ads work differently depending on the selling situation.

> *Ads work differently depending on the selling situation.*

Rossiter and Percy in their book *Advertising Communications and
Promotion Management*[3] discuss their expanded version of the FCB grid
in great detail. Buy their book and maybe you won't be victimized the
way Covad victimized itself. The following discussion is based in large
part on Rossiter and Percy's original presentation and elaboration of the
FCB framework.

The first challenge is brand awareness. If the customer does not
remember the Covad name, then it is rather difficult for the customer to take any sort of action that will stimulate Covad's business.
Spending the last two or three seconds of the commercial on their
"just revamped" brand name will achieve very little. There are too
many people out there who do not sit on the edge of their seats when
watching commercials.

*Brand awareness is the first challenge.*

There are two types of brand awareness: recall and recognition. Most products sold in grocery stores can rely on recognition. Consumers wander the aisles and stop and drop in their baskets a product they recognize, rather than one they have never seen or heard about before. If you stop them and tell them to close their eyes and list the brand names of all the products in their basket, you will be surprised how often they know it's that "tall green" whatchamacallit, but can't think of the name just then.

In other situations, it may be necessary for the customer to ask for the product. For example, since Covad's services are sold through Internet service providers (ISPs), the imagined sales scenario is one in which prospective Covad end customers contact their ISPs to ask about Covad. Recognition works for toilet paper; it does not work for broadband.

*There are two types of brand awareness: recall and recognition.*

There are different advertisement rules for recognition or recall. Some examples of key rules are as follows:

**For brand recognition:**

1. Ensure sufficient exposure of the brand package and the name in the ad. European ads used to fail dismally here. Typically there would be a minute of highly creative scenes with no connection to anything, then two seconds showing the product and the name. Advertisers seemed a little ashamed to be advertisers.
2. The category need should be mentioned or portrayed unless immediately obvious. No need to explain the use of toilet paper, but broadband by Covad in 1999 is a very different matter.
3. After the initial burst, less media frequency is needed for brand recognition.

### For brand recall

1. Associate the category need and the brand in the main copy line and include a personal reference. Covad's tag line was, "The Internet as it should be." It should have said, "<u>Covad</u> brings *you* the Internet as it should be."
2. Use repetition of the main copy line for recall. When recalling a name or phone number, repetition is key. You don't stare at a phone number. You repeat a phone number in your mind. In contrast, if you want to recognize a face or image, you stare at it to imprint it on your brain.
3. Keep up your advertising frequency. Recall goes down much faster than recognition.

---

*Advertisement rules are different for recognition or recall.*

---

Brand awareness is the first challenge. Brand attitude is the second challenge. With brand attitude we are concerned about how customers evaluate the brand they are made aware of. Products are classified in a two-by-two matrix along two dimensions: importance of the product decision to the customer and the motivation to buy.

For many cheap and simple products the purchase decision is not important to most of us, or we have already purchased the item many times, and therefore we will not look for helpful information in advertisements (think toilet paper, beer, aspirin). For products that are sufficiently new or complex or risky, however, the purchase decision is more important, and we do look for helpful information in advertisements (think Covad, a car, a new restaurant).

Next, some products we buy from what I call a negative motivation: aspirin, plumbing repairs, life insurance. Other products are bought from a positive motivation: perfume, a new car, a soft drink, a movie.

Note that for some products different customers will have different perspectives on the importance or motivation of the purchasing decision. A candy purchase for my youngest sons is a very high-importance, positive-motivation decision. A candy purchase for a 50-year-old trying to lose weight could be a low-importance, negative-motivation decision. The chart below gives examples of products in four quadrants, based on the importance/motivation classification that would apply to most purchasers.

Selling situations: motivation versus importance

Motivation

| | Negative | Positive |
|---|---|---|
| **High** | I<br><br>Dentist<br><br>Life insurance | II<br><br>Sports car<br><br>Hair coloring |
| **Importance** | III<br><br>Razor<br><br>Aspirin | IV<br><br>Beer<br><br>Cigarettes |

Low

The rules for what makes a good advertisement are different for the four different selling situations. Does sex or humor sell? Should you wildly exaggerate the benefits of your product? Should the product or the customer be the "hero" in the ad? Should you provide lots of explicit information or emphasize the brand image? The answers to these questions depend on the selling situation. Much of it is common sense. Do you want the PDA favored by famous actresses? Anyone for a hilarious headache commercial?

Below are some specific examples of different rules of advertising in different quadrants. I do not attempt to provide the full set of rules and justifications and underlying research findings. My main goal is to intrigue you and alert you to the fact that there is well-researched stuff worth knowing that your marketing managers, advertising managers, and advertising agencies may be blissfully unaware of.

> *Different rules of advertising apply for different products. Make sure your advertising manager and advertising agency know this.*

## Quadrant I: High importance/ negative motivation

1. Correct emotional portrayal – anger, fear, disappointment, guilt, mild annoyance – consistent with the buying motivation is important early in the product life cycle, less important later on. Covad portrays anger. But is the prospective customer angry? Is the motivation to get Covad negative? I don't know. I doubt it. I suspect that Covad and its ad agency don't even know that they should worry about this.

2. The target audience has to accept the main points, but in contrast to ads for products bought with positive motivation, does not have to like the ad itself. Advertisements for dentists or lawyers or life insurance shouldn't be funny, clever, or visually stunning. Life insurance is associated with death. Don't use a funny duck as your spokesperson. In contrast, auto insurance is associated with getting a car. You can be funny.

2. The target audience's initial attitude toward the brand must be the overriding consideration. After the *Valdez* incident in Alaska when Exxon was not so popular, Exxon had to explicitly address pollution issues in its advertisements – or not advertise at all. Don't ignore what your target audience is thinking. You are not a carnival barker. In this quadrant you are in a conversation with your customers.

## Quadrant II: High importance/ positive motivation

1. Emotional authenticity is paramount. Is the target audience elated, excited, flattered, proud? The advertisement should be tailored to lifestyle groups within the audience. A Mercedes Benz buyer is a proud pillar of the community. A Corvette buyer is an elated member of the "cool guys with money" fraternity. A Porsche buyer combines pride and elation. I speculate that "excited" and membership in an "always on, connected, high-tech" lifestyle group is the emotional status of someone interested in getting Covad.

2. People must identify personally with the product as portrayed in the ad and not merely like the ad. The Joe Isuzu ads may run into a little problem here. Likable and funny ad, no doubt, but will I identify personally with Isuzu by way of a funny, lying car salesman?

3. Provide information when the audience lacks information. As mentioned earlier, advertising agencies argue that nobody reads ads. This is

because advertising agencies don't read ads since they are not interested in the product.

4. Overclaiming is recommended but do not underclaim. You see an automobile ad for a boring little econobox deeply admired by a short-skirted female cyclist stopping to turn and stare. You might think the ad a bit unbelievable, but to the buyer this is a major purchase, and he (or she) does feel everybody will be looking in admiration.

### Quadrant III: Low importance/negative emotion

1. Use a simple problem solution format: "This stain will never get out. Surprise, Tide did get the stain out." Procter & Gamble knows its marketing better than most any other company, and one thing it does is keep its advertising to the point: simple and predictable. There is nothing wrong with simple and predictable. Stay true to your message, keep your customers, and earn your returns. Look for excitement when you go spending your money; earning is serious business.

2. It is not necessary for people to like the ad. Commercials for headache remedies tend to give you a headache rather than entertain you. We don't use the headache remedy with the brand personality that we like or that fits our lifestyle or that is preferred by famous actresses. Rather, we use the headache remedy that works.

3. Benefit claims should be stated extremely. Headaches disappear in a matter of minutes if not seconds. A zit and you have to go out tonight? No problem, Clearasil delivers. People know the ads exaggerate. But if one headache remedy says it works in ten seconds, and another says it will take one minute, which one do you buy?

### Quadrant IV: Low importance/positive emotion

1. Emotional authenticity is the key element and is the single determinant benefit. You are the cola you drink, the beer you drink. I read once that young staffers at the Clinton White House all drank Diet Coke. Coke Classic full of sugar is somehow perceived as anti-environmental, anti-intellectual, Republican.

2. The execution of the emotion must be unique to the brand. Marlboro is a good example. The cowboy as cigarette smoker is so uniquely Marlboro that just the picture of a man on a horse riding through beautiful nature is enough to get quitters to take up smoking again.

3. The target audience must like the ad. Coca-Cola, Pepsi, Marlboro – all have highly likable ads with likable, beautiful people. For products

such as these, sex and humor pay off. They don't pay off for you when you sell detergent or aspirin.

4. The delivery of the brand message is by association and is often implicit. Note how Virgina Slims' "You've come a long way, baby" shows its pencil-thin models holding the pencil-thin cigarette and thereby *implicitly* conveys its key selling point: smoking keeps your weight down. I fear lots of teenage girls will prefer to be thin and die at 60, rather than be fat and die at 70. The ads also *associate* Virginia Slims with tennis, with health and with bright white tennis clothes, thereby *implicitly* contradicting concerns about yellow fingers, lungs, and teeth. Implicit messages, compared to explicit messages, side-step counter arguments by the audience. If you explicitly argued that Virginia Slims make you more sporty, people would not accept the message. Given the low importance of the product, however, we are able to sneak though with an implicit message.

> *Know your selling situation and the rules of advertising for your selling situation.*

Much greater detail on the above is found in John Rossiter and Larry Percy's book. No point in rewriting the book here, good as it may be. It is clear that to leave the design of your advertising up to "creatives" without consideration or knowledge even of the motivation and involvement of the target audience and the implications thereof is not a good idea.

How about Covad? We won't know without testing, but I suspect that an ad of an excited Covad user showing an impressed friend how well the Internet works with Covad, explaining to the friend how Covad works and most importantly, what to do to get Covad ("Contact your ISP and ask about Covad") might have worked better. Ah, but it is difficult to explain how it works? Of course it is difficult to explain, so you should use maybe a 60-second commercial or a two-minute commercial – otherwise you stay away from TV.

Maybe you should use only direct mail. Talk to your strategic communications partner – the advertising agency – about this thought. See how objectively they help you to consider this alternative communications approach. See how they start mumbling. This is why direct mail is done mostly by independent agencies. Advertising agencies can't bring themselves to do it when the post office doesn't give them a percentage of the stamps that are sold (now there's an idea for the Post Office!).

## Breaking the rules

"We like to break the rules. We are the wild and crazy guys." So boast the creative directors of the ad agency. The truth is that too many people who work for advertising agencies have no clue what the rules are. They pride themselves on out-of-the-box thinking, but they really specialize in I've-never-heard-of-the-box thinking. In your next conversation with your agency, see if they have any knowledge of the FCB model.

But breaking the rules is good, right? Imagine a car race through a busy city. The winner will race through green and proceed through red whenever it seems safe enough to do so. Here, deliberately breaking the rules is no sin. Second will be the one who stops for all red lights and races through green lights. Last to arrive, or not at all, is the one who doesn't know about red lights or green lights. Breaking rules? How do you do it when you don't know it when you do it?

Professor Scott Armstrong from the Wharton School, University of Pennsylvania, has published a book entitled *Persuasive Advertising* (see Note 1). The book is unique in that it assembles all known empirical research past and present on what makes a good advertisement. The book naturally entailed an enormous amount of work by a team of researchers. Reading the book requires some dedication too. Professor Armstrong explains: "The question for you is whether you think cumulative knowledge from experts, typical practice, and research can add to your current knowledge."

Some practitioners I have worked with would answer a resounding "No" to Armstrong's question. I understand why someone would not want to put in the effort to read the book. But I don't understand why a company would hire someone to do their advertising who cannot be bothered to educate him- or herself about advertising. Would you hire a doctor who has no interest in finding out which treatments work better to treat your disease, and which treatments don't work at all or might make matters worse?

*Learn the rules first so you can break them properly– (Mark Twain).*

Another rule-breaking campaign by a company I forget for a detergent I forget – now there is a great campaign – attracted a lot of admiring press with a lifestyle-type commercial featuring the song, "Put On Your Red Dress Mamma, 'Cause You're Going Out Tonight."[4]

The ad shows Mamma looking for her red dress, only to find her daughter hiding under the bed, daughter and dress smeared with makeup. She laughs (as mothers will when their little daughters smear makeup over the favorite dress mother plans to wear that evening). And, surprise, the detergent saves the day. The final shot, with the box of detergent standing silently but meaningfully on the table, shows Mom and exceedingly handsome Dad leaving for their dinner date. The implicit message: use this detergent and you will be beautiful and you will have a beautiful husband who takes you out for dinner. Nice commercial if you sell perfume; positively rule-breaking if you sell detergent.

Great commercial, great music, my students had all seen it. And none of them knew the company or the brand. Granted, students are not detergent-buying housewives, but I haven't seen too many more campaigns suggesting that the right choice of detergent will get you a handsome man.

You are what you drive, you are what you smoke, you are what you drink, you are what you wear – but you are *not* the detergent you wash your clothes with.

> *You are what you drink, smoke, or wear, but you are not the detergent you wash your clothes with.*

One more rule-breaker: an advertisement for a new and very expensive, somewhat technical product. The headline in this advertisement says "Tracking a Package Shouldn't Be Easier Than Tracking a Person." The picture shows a row of apartment blocks at the end of a dirt road in a nondescript place. There is a dog on the dirt road.

Advertisement? For what? What does the slogan mean? What is the ad trying to say? To whom is it trying to appeal? Who feels strongly that a package, relative to a person, is found too easily? What is this company selling? Is this Federal Express maybe, or the Post Office? What is the dog doing in the ad? Tracking a person or a package?

The advertiser is Iridium, a consortium of companies led by Motorola, selling satellite phones. Where are these phones? What do they look like? What do they cost? Where can I buy one? Why should I buy one? What are the advantages? What are the disadvantages? Why are the phones not shown? I have shown the ad many times – once to a room full of Motorola managers – and it always takes a long time before even one person figures out that this is an ad for a phone by Iridium.

Does the advertising agency think I will become so desirous of owning a satellite phone by this intriguing advertisement that no information is needed? The campaign included some airport advertising on big billboards. These billboards said "Iridium." What is the theory here? That people will become very curious, start looking in phone books and calling their friends? Iridium's company magazine *Roam* reported excitedly that staffers started calling in from all corners of the world about having seen the ads. A beautiful example of a company talking to itself.[5]

It's also an example of how so many technical companies are far better at making products than at making advertisements. Maybe the engineers running technical companies don't feel comfortable challenging their creative advertising agencies and advertising managers.[6]

> *If your advertising doesn't make sense to you, it won't make sense to anybody.*

## ✍ POINTS TO REMEMBER

- ☛ Ads work differently depending on the selling situation.
- ☛ Brand awareness is the first challenge.
- ☛ There are two types of brand awareness: recall and recognition.
- ☛ Advertisement rules are different for recognition or recall.
- ☛ Different rules of advertising apply for different products. Make sure your advertising manager and advertising agency know this.
- ☛ Know your selling situation and the rules of advertising for your selling situation.
- ☛ Learn the rules first so you can break them properly— (Mark Twain).
- ☛ You are what you drink, smoke, or wear, but you are not the detergent you wash your clothes with.
- ☛ If your advertising doesn't make sense to you, it won't make sense to anybody.

# Notes

1. Scott Armstrong, *Persuasive Advertising* (Palgrave Macmillan, 2008).
2. See Richard Vaughn (1983), "How Advertising Works: A Planning Model," *Journal of Advertising Research*, Vol. 23, pp. 22–8, and Richard Vaughn (1986), "How Advertising Works: A Planning Model Revisited," *Journal of Advertising Research* (February/March), pp. 57–66.
3. John R. Rossiter and Larry Percy, *Advertising Communications and Promotion Management* (McGraw-Hill, 1997).
4. The lines are from Tommy Tucker's song The detergent was Fresh Start laundry detergent.
5. Customers were less excited. After three months, the US$ 180 million global advertising campaign had sold about 150 phones per satellite. Those are the kinds of numbers to make a grown man cry.
6. Motorola is not an exception. According to a 2001 study by Ipsos-ASI: "Copy Testing U.S.-Style," *www.ipsos-ideas.com* (23 August 2003), only 45 of the largest 100 advertisers in the U.S. in 2001 regularly tested copy of their advertisements prior to running the full advertising campaign. None of the seven telecommunications companies in this select group of big spenders regularly pre-tested their advertisements, while 25 of 27 fmcg (fast moving consumer goods) companies regularly pre-tested. Rhetorical question for marketing VPs in telecommunications companies: can the fmcg companies learn a thing or two from you about advertising; that's why they need to test and you don't?

# 11 Media Selection: Where Should You Advertise?

### Key messages to whet your appetite

▶ People live in media land
▶ People live in tribes
▶ Media – message – execution

## The neighborhood you live in

*People now live in media land. They don't sit on the front porch talking to the neighbors; they sit inside and talk to their TV, nod at their newspaper, rant at their computer. Products and communication are distributed nationwide, even globally. But that does not mean they are everywhere. It just means that geography has lost meaning as a variable. Geographically speaking, your customers can live anywhere. In terms of media, they do not live anywhere. They live in traditional newspapers, or network television, or cable, and so on. Western civilizations have fallen apart into different tribes. But these modern tribes do not live on this or that side of the Rhine; they live on this or that side of various media divides. Media selection means deciding where you will live. It's a big question. This chapter offers some practical tools to answer that big question.*

## Direct matching

Direct matching is a technique for media selection that works by presenting surveys with lists of TV programs, radio stations, and magazines to current and potential customers, and asking them to check off TV programs they watch frequently, radio stations they listen to frequently, and magazines or newspapers they read frequently. In this manner you can identify programs watched by your current customers, competitors' customers, brand switchers, non-users, and even ex-users.

You will find TV programs, magazines and newspapers that are popular across different groups, you will also find media options that are popular with one group but not the other. You will find, for example, some television programs that are heavily watched by your customers, and some programs that are heavily watched by the customers of one or another competing brand. You can run different campaigns with different messages for different groups: "Try us, you'll like us!" for competitors' customers and non-users; "Use the brand you trust!" for our customers; "Use only us!" for brand switchers. Just make sure you use direct matching to connect your different user groups with different media options.

> *Where to advertise? Ask your (prospective) customers.*

You can also save a lot of money by using direct matching. I did direct matching for a franchising company, Dial One, in 1993. Homeowners in need of home repair services, security systems, swimming pools and such were the target audience. I found that in New Orleans 1 percent of homeowners could be reached weekly for an average cost of $24.73 across the 27 different TV programs the company had advertised on the year before. The cost ranged from $6.94 on the Channel 8 news programs between 6 and 7 am to $42.37 on *Cops* at 6:30 pm. Obviously huge savings are possible by investigating media consumption specifically for your target market.

Brooklyn Industries, a new, very cool clothing store chain in New York, advertised in very cool magazines that you and I have never heard of ,such as BPM or L (well, maybe you heard of them, but I hadn't). Brooklyn did some direct matching research (talked to its customers) and discovered their cool customers also never read these cool magazines. They read *The New York Times*. In any case, most customers knew Brooklyn not from its ads, but from seeing its stores. Brooklyn decided to spend its advertising money on nicer window displays.[1] Some "street furniture" advertising on garbage cans and bus stops within a mile radius of the stores might be good too.

"Direct matching" is what we call the media selection technique where you ask current and potential customers directly about their media consumption. The traditional approach to media selection is referred to as "demographic matching."

## Demographic matching

Demographic (indirect) matching involves two steps. First, you identify your customers' gender, age, income and education. You come up with a description of your market target as "men between the ages of 30 and 45" because your research shows you that 80 percent of your customers are indeed men between the ages of 30 and 45.

Second, with the help of your advertising agency you identify, say, ten TV programs that most economically deliver the desired demographics. Suppose each of these programs is watched by about 10 percent of men between the ages of 30 and 45. If you buy ten advertisements on each program, all men will have seen your ad ten times, provided there is no overlap of audiences between the ten programs.

But there is always overlap. How much overlap? How many men who watch program number one also watch program number two? Last time I asked a TV station to provide me this information, it told me it did not have such data. This is interesting because when Nielsen collects the data, it knows how many men who watch program one also watch two, and so forth.

In the study for Dial One, I found that about 10 percent of the target audience had watched about 50 percent of all advertising the company had run during the previous year, and another 20 percent had watched another 40 percent of all advertisements. Overlap was very high, and this may well be why the TV industry has no desire to tell you about it. Overlap causes waste when we advertise to the same man – probably a man with no job or money – over and over again. This is one important reason why direct matching is better.

> *Don't advertise to the same customer over and over.*

But overlap is not the only source of waste. Another source of waste occurs when that man who watches your advertising over and over again is not a current or potential buyer; he just fits your demographic profile of a desirable customer.

It may well be that 80 percent of people buying automatics rifles are men between the ages of 30 and 45. But what percentage of men between the ages of 30 and 45 buys automatic rifles? Suppose 4 percent of men between the ages of 30 and 45 are potential customers for automatic rifles. Then even if 100 percent of the audience of a program consists of men between the ages of 30 and 45, you still waste 96 percent of your money when you advertise on that program.

This is why direct matching is better; matching *your customers or potential customers*, regardless of age, gender, income, or education, directly to different programs, rather than indirectly through demographics.

The same story applies to radio advertising, newspaper advertising, direct mail, and magazine advertising. If your best option to reach your particular audience is *Fortune*, then whether *Forbes, Business Week, Inc.*, or Fox News at 6 pm is your next best option depends on the overlap for your particular audience of *Fortune* with those additional choices. And you may find that any additional magazine is not worth it, so you should shift to another medium.

In the case of Dial One, I built a new TV media schedule for the company by selecting first the program that gave us the most target customers (putting extra weight on high-potential customers) for the least money. Then I selected the next program, but subtracted points for overlap, giving only half credit for reaching customers who had already been reached through the first program. Then I selected the next program, giving only half credit for customers who had been reached through either of the first two programs, and a one-fourth credit for those who had already been reached through both the previous programs. I followed a similar procedure for the fourth and fifth program selected. But on this basis the fifth program already was no longer cost effective. The fifth program was mostly an uneconomical way to reach people we had reached before. The company concentrated its advertising spending on just those four programs and was able to reach more homeowners more often than before at the same cost. (Alternatively it could have cut its budget by 30 percent and achieved the same results as before.)

The effectiveness of any particular media vehicle (TV, radio, magazines, newspaper, billboards, direct mail, and the Internet) drops rapidly with the choice of additional venues (additional programs on TV, ads in the newspaper, and so forth) within the same vehicle. You must compare the added frequency and reach delivered by using additional vehicles relative to using additional venues within the same vehicle. Remember too that spending time and money to make sure your advertisements appear in the right place is much cheaper than running your advertisements in the wrong place.

> *Overlap and waste are more likely when you concentrate your money on a single vehicle.*

Another reason to spend money in complementary media vehicles is that seeing an advertisement on TV and then in a magazine provides a more powerful media experience for your target customer than seeing the same ad on TV twice. If you receive the same message from two different sources it is more believable – much like hearing a recommendation for a new restaurant from two friends rather than twice from the same friend.

Finally, an important advantage of direct matching is that it allows you to define your target audience in any way you like. As I mentioned in Chapter 6, traditionally you are not supposed to define your market as, say, "optimistic people," since you cannot buy media space based on that definition. But that is only true if you use traditional demographic matching. If you use direct matching you can define your market as "optimistic people" (or as anything else) and then use surveys to identify such people and the media that best reach them.[2]

## Direct matching is not so popular

Direct matching requires that your marketing manager knows about marketing and is willing to spend the extra effort to do direct matching. Alternatively, you need an advertising agency that not only knows about advertising but is also willing to put in the effort to educate you. Thus we are not surprised that direct matching is not popular. Through direct matching you can achieve your communication goals with less money.

Wisconsin car dealer Russ Darrow took the lead among Republican candidates running for a senate seat in Wisconsin by using cable TV, the ultimate direct-matching tool. His competitors followed the traditional, lazy way of throwing money at broadcast advertising, the fastest way for political consultants to spend/collect cash. Mr. Darrow put $250,000 of ads on just Fox News, MSNBC, and CNBC in just ten counties, containing 50 percent of the Republican vote, among 72 counties in Wisconsin. As a result he jumped from 25 percent to 40 percent in polls of Republican voters. Why did his competitors not use cable? It's a shameful fact that political campaigns allocated less than 10 percent of their TV-ad dollars to cable TV because it was "difficult to negotiate with multiple cable operators and cable channels."[3] Don't let your marketing managers or your advertising agencies waste your money because it is the easier and faster way for them to make more money. Media selection receives less attention than the message. The message receives less attention than the creative execution. You should reverse this order of attention.

> *Get your priorities straight: media – message – execution.*

---

### ✍ POINTS TO REMEMBER

☞ **Where to advertise? Ask your (prospective) customers.**

☞ **Don't advertise to the same customer over and over.**

☞ **Overlap and waste are more likely when you concentrate your money on a single vehicle.**

☞ **Get your priorities straight: media – message – execution.**

---

## Notes

1. Beth Kwon, "One Company's Budget: Sales More Than Doubled Last Year. So Why Are They Changing Tactics?" *Inc.* (January 2007), p. 54.
2. A further detailed discussion of direct versus demographic matching can be found in John R. Rossiter and Larry Percy, *Advertising Communications and Promotion Management* (McGraw-Hill, 1997).
3. Cynthia H. Cho and Julia Angwin, "Politicians Find Cable Efficient Way to Target Voters," *The Wall Street Journal* (4 August 2004), B1, B3.

# 12 Your Advertising Agency Is Not Your Partner

---

## Key messages to whet your appetite

▶ Your advertising agency is not your strategic communications partner.
▶ Use more than one ad agency.
▶ Test creative executions against one another.

---

## Advertising agencies

*Some of my best friends work in advertising agencies. Since this chapter is so unkind to advertising agencies I tell them to skip this chapter. This way I can keep my friends. If you work for an ad agency, you too can skip this chapter. You already know what's in it anyway. Everybody else, please pay close attention. Managing your advertising agency is an important issue. Advertising is your mouth. I'm not sure companies should outsource their mouth, but they do.*

*When you outsource you need to manage your advertising agency closely and carefully. You may need their expertise, but you better make sure first that they have some expertise. Further, be aware always that your advertising agency's interests are not aligned with your interests. Can advertising agencies add value to your business? If you manage them well, they can add great value. If you don't manage them carefully, you might get lucky, but more likely your advertising effort won't be nearly as good as it could have been if you'd just done the job yourself.*

## Advertising agencies exist to help themselves, not you

Remember that you cannot rely on your advertising agency to judge your ad. Also, you cannot rely on your ad agency to create the best possible ad for your product. To the ad agency, any ad is also an ad for the agency.

When creatives in the agency design your ad for you, they are inevitably thinking about how your ad will enhance their portfolio of creative work to show to a prospective employer. This is why agencies and their creatives have a strong bias to "advertise the ad" rather than the product. Look at your advertisements and ask yourself how much space and time is given over to the product and how much to the ad.

When managers for advertising agencies attend my seminars, they strongly disagree with me on this point, but incentives rule behavior and perceptions – whether we like it or not. Self-interest drives beliefs. It is part of the human condition, and advertising agencies in this regard are no different from the rest of us. Note, for example, that global advertising agencies argue in favor of global advertising, while local agencies believe in localized advertising.

> *If you trust your advertising agency, you will get what you deserve – which is nothing.*

Another issue is that entirely too many companies create a contest between agencies to decide which agency they will use. The agencies then fall all over themselves to show how creative they are. Creativity, this magical thing, is their competitive advantage. Effectiveness does not come into play at all at this stage. The agencies participate in a beauty contest in which each agency gets one morning or afternoon to show its stuff. Balloons, marching bands, dancing girls and whatnot are hauled in to show the creative excitement capability of the agency. Managers and agency executives are all on the edge of their seats, not a customer in sight. It's enough to make me want to cry.

Going back to our earlier discussion of Motorola's advertising campaign for its satellite phone venture, how did Iridium find its agency (Ammirati Puris Lintas) to create its beautiful ads? *The Wall Street Journal Europe* reports:[1]

> "We are a hothouse of world-changing ideas," said Saatchi & Saatchi chairwoman Jennifer Laing, offering a "Master Brand Temple" and a brand management tool billed as B-rand, R-esources, A-dvertising, I-nformation, and N-etwork.

Fallon McElligot passed out piles of modeling clay, mangled by focus groups of travelers. The lumps showed travelers' anger at technology, Chairman Pat Fallon explained.

For its pitch, APL [presented] an analysis of 600 global travelers ... "They feel they are the chosen ones in the company: special, tougher, with greater endurance," APL's Robert Quish said. But paradoxically, Mr. Quish went on, they also worry that people will think them frauds, or that they will miss out on critical office politics while on the road, or that their children will reject them for their absenteeism. Tap into their worries, offer control, reassurance and snob appeal and Iridium will win, Mr. Quish pitched.

APL won the account and its New York office came up with the winning creative design: "a series of mysterious photographs and slogans designed to both flatter and frighten the powerful."

Flatter and frighten? How about selling a phone? The contempt for the audience – all those frightened executives in business and first class – is palpable. The wild overestimation of an advertisement's impact is beyond laughable. The advertisements do not address senior business executives; they address the advertising agency's warped idea of senior business executives. After five months, the Iridium advertising campaign had flattered and frightened about 150 customers per satellite into buying a phone, about one customer per $15,000 advertising. Nice job, Ammirati Puris Lintas. Did you ask those executives in your survey how often they are in areas without cellular phone access? Two answers come to mind: rarely and never.

Yet we should not blame Ammirati Puris Lintas. They simply did what they had to do to land the account, and they did land the account, and they made a lot of money. They didn't make the rules of the game of how advertising agencies are selected. We have to blame the customer – in this case Iridium. It is amazing that companies let advertising agencies do marketing research as part of the "pitching" exercise, probably figuring they get something for nothing (free research from several advertising agencies).

> *Free research from your ad agency is not worth what you pay for it.*

Iridium spent billions of dollars developing and building a global satellite phone network and tried to avoid spending any money on researching potential markets and alternative marketing methods. Here is one crazy thought: maybe Iridium should have used a market research agency to do market research. Even crazier thought: maybe Iridium itself should have talked to potential customers and passed out those lumps of clay.

Iridium is not atypical though. Howard Schultz, the founder of Starbucks, relates in his book *Pour Your Heart Into It*[2] how he decided to start advertising Starbucks on national television. "A team of us first met with all four [advertising agencies], and I explained my goals for Starbucks. They did market research…and they uncovered a disturbing theme…we had not told our story well enough."

I have to smile. What a surprise. Four advertising agencies each do market research for Starbucks and all four come to the same conclusion: Starbucks needs to do a lot of advertising. I mean, what are the odds, right?

In fairness, you can't expect an advertising agency, investing serious money in its effort to land an account, to come back and tell a potential customer that its intended marketing strategy is deeply flawed, that maybe owners of large boats are a better target when you want to sell satellite phones. (Satellite phones don't really work inside buildings and they were big as a brick. They are useless, cumbersome, and unnecessary when you go to Tokyo or Frankfurt. But they look great and certainly are impressive when you are offshore on your yacht.) Do you expect advertising agencies to do market research and inform you that an expensive TV advertising campaign is not the best way to proceed?

Advertising agencies will talk about being your strategic communications partner. One internal document by an agency proclaims, "We want to go to bed with our customers and we want to get up with our customers. We want to be there when the decisions are made." This is good for the agency, but it is not good for you.

The advertising agency is no more your strategic communications partner than a car salesman is your strategic transportation partner, or a stockbroker your strategic investment partner.

> *The advertising agency is no more your strategic communications partner than a car salesman is your strategic transportation partner.*

## How many advertising agencies do you have?

Quaker Oats, after World War II, was one of the first companies to take the then radical step of employing more than one advertising agency.[3] Sony similarly spreads its advertising work across several agencies, believing – don't know where they got such a notion – that competition is an incentive for better performance.[4]

McDonald's, one of the most consistently innovative advertisers ever, traditionally uses as many as 50 advertising agencies. Franchisee associations in major cities are free to use their own agency and run their own ads. When any advertisement proves successful additional franchisee groups are quick to adopt. Local agencies can look forward to a bonanza in dollars and fame when their creative idea proves successful. Most of McDonald's advertising innovations, such as using TV to advertise its restaurants, advertising to children, using a clown as a spokesperson, came from individual franchisees working closely with local agencies.[5]

> *Don't use just one advertising agency.*

An extreme form of using many competing creative agents is the new trend of user-generated ads. Of course, these users are not your average users. Some of them will be hobbyists or professionals seizing the chance to display their talent on a national platform. Can the creative department of one agency really outshine all such competitors?[6] "We are pros, and although it looks easy to create advertising, it isn't. User-generated content reminds me there's a reason I have a job," writes Wayne Best, executive creative director of New York boutique agency TAXI, in an e-mail to Jon Fine at *Business Week*.[7] There may be a good reason that Wayne Best has his job, but he is a special case according to Graham Phillips, former CEO of Ogilvy and Mather: "Too much of today's advertising is irrelevant and a waste of money. Ten years ago, some observers opined that ad agencies seemed more interested in selling their product than the client's product. Since then, it has gone from bad to worse."[8]

Because the buzz mistakenly is all about user-generated advertising, about passionate consumers who create ads for products they love, the thinking is that this sort of thing will not work for products that generate no passion. Jon Fine argues that soap is not exciting and that it is unlikely that soap buyers will make ads for soap. I suspect he is right. Soap buyers will not submit ads out of passion. Soap buyers might not even submit ads in hopes of winning a prize of say US$10,000 or 100,000. But plenty of advertising professionals and amateurs alike will love to submit ads in hopes of being selected and winning that $100,000. Any smart company today spending more than even a few million dollars on advertising should organize contests to see if the contests can generate an ad that beats the best efforts of its ad agency (if nothing else, it'll make your ad agency work just a little harder).

> *Use contests to get better creative work for your ads.*

I suggested a contest for user-generated ads to a company while I was meeting with the company and its advertising agency. The reaction of the ad agency representatives was most entertaining. Any warm feelings were definitely out of the window. They scoffed at the idea and pointed out the cost of publicizing the contest. It's nice to hear an ad agency worry about its client's costs of communication for a change. But that cost is small, plus the contest itself is promotion for your company and its products, even if you were to get no creative work out of it. If you offer a $100,000 prize you just need to do a press release and announce the offer on your website. Maybe send e-mails to a few film schools and advertising schools. Word will spread fast. You might get creative work from countries you have never even heard of. Even if the contest does not beat your agency, your agency will be obliged to work harder for its money. That's probably why they hate this idea.

Poor Philips Electronics unfortunately (because I own stock in the company) still relies on just one agency.[9] Philips advertisements traditionally hide its products, allocating most space to some cool guy or a cute baby. As Philips moved from "making things better" to "sense and simplicity," its ads became simpler, but Philips still is too ashamed of its products to want to show them to you, they still advertise their advertising agency's creativity more than they advertise their products. Should you show the product or should you show the customer in your ad? Tests of ads for consumer electronics show that you should give pride of place to your product.[10] I have done such tests in seminars, including seminars with Philips and with Sony, always yielding the same results: if you want to sell a video camera or a TV, show the camera, show the TV, don't show a cute child or a cool guy. Perhaps if Philips used ad ideas from many different sources and tested the results they might start advertising Philips rather than cool guys and cute babies. The stock would go up.

> *Test different creative executions against one another.*

> ✍   **POINTS TO REMEMBER**
>
> ☞ **If you trust your advertising agency, you will get what you deserve – which is nothing.**
> ☞ **Free research from your ad agency is not worth what you pay for it.**
> ☞ **The advertising agency is no more your strategic communications partner than a car salesman is your strategic transportation partner.**
> ☞ **Don't use just one advertising agency.**
> ☞ **Use contests to get better creative work for your ads.**
> ☞ **Test different creative executions against one another.**

## Notes

1. Quentin Hardy, "Iridium's Orbit: For a World Phone, Pitch Plays on Fears Of Being Isolated – Satellite Consortium Opts For That Line to Build Global Brand Overnight – Beaming Logo on Clouds," *The Wall Street Journal Europe* (4 June 1998).
2. Howard Schultz and Dori Jones Yang, *Pour Your Heart Into It* (Hyperion, 1997), p. 263.
3. See the International Directory of Company Histories by the Gale Group, Inc., Topics from Answers.com, 2007.
4. Evan Ramstead and Geoffrey Fowler, "At Samsung, It's Crunch Time for Ad Strategy – Agency Review May Shape Firm's Ability to Compete Under New Marketing Chief," *The Asian Wall Street Journal* (7 September 2004).
5. John. F. Love, *McDonald's: Behind The Arches* (Bantam, 1995).
6. Julie Bosmanan, "Agency's Worst Nightmare: Ads Created by Users," *The New York Times, Media & Advertising* (11 May 2006), D1.
7. Jon Fine, "What Makes 'Citizen Ads' Work," *Business Week* (19 February 2007), p. 24. Jon Fine also writes a great blog on advertising and media, http://www.businessweek.com/innovate/FineOnMedia
8. "Let's Fix Advertising," *Advertising Age* (20 May 2002), p. 26.
9. Ramstead and Fowler, "At Samsung, It's Crunch Time for Ad Strategy."
10. Philip Ward Burton and Scott C. Purvis, *Which Ad Pulled Best?* (NTC Business Books, 1996).

# 13   Ask Not What Your Brand Can Do For You ...

**Key messages to whet your appetite**

▶ Brand value comes from value to customers
▶ Your product and your service create your brand
▶ Watch out for engineers who read marketing books
▶ When brand is important, you must be your brand

## The valuable brand

*In discussions of branding, there is rare mention of the value of a brand for customers. The term 'brand value' refers to the value of the brand for the seller, not the buyer. Yet, only when a brand delivers value to buyers can it deliver value to sellers.*

*I was invited recently to attend a presentation by an advertising agency on a new brand strategy for a furniture manufacturer. There were beautiful slides. Famous names such as Dell and Starbucks and Amazon were thrown around. Lessons from such powerhouse brand names were put forth on nice PowerPoint slides with arrows and boxes linking concepts such as cost control, customer this, and product that.*

*Only one thing was missing. The agency presentation was all about communication. Yet there was nothing to be communicated. There was no mention of what the new brand would deliver for the customer. So in my discussion of branding in this chapter I look, first, at the ways brands deliver value to customers. Then I discuss how brands deliver value to companies.*

# Ask what your brand can do for your customer!

First, a brand can make decision-making easier for customers. McDonald's is not a fine dining restaurant, but it is one of the strongest restaurant brands in the world. When you go to Jakarta, Beijing, Tokyo or Madrid, sooner or later you might eat at McDonald's for no other reason than that you recognize the logo and know what they have for you. McDonald's as a brand, and its various sub-brands such as Big Mac and Happy Meal, reduce the cost of decision-making when you wish to eat outside of your home. We eat at McDonald's not because we necessarily love the food more, but because we like the familiarity more, because it is easier.

McDonald's, in a way, is like Mom's home cooking, assuming you still had a mom who cooked at home. Mom may not be the greatest cook in the world, but you have to eat what she puts on your plate, and it is not going to be surprising, and there is some comfort and happiness in that too. The brand delivers convenience not just of cooking for you and doing your dishes (kind of), but also of taking away the work of searching for a restaurant, evaluating its menu, making sure it is not a tourist rip-off place, deciding what to eat, and so on.

> *Brands can make decision-making easier.*

Second, for many products I cannot easily judge the quality, maybe not even after I purchased and used the product. That's why people say: "I'm going get me the most expensive lawyer in town." Nobody wants the cheapest surgeon in town either. The same is true when we buy wine or cosmetics or medicine. If it is very expensive there is a better chance it's a good product. When I buy from a famous company I assume I run less risk of being cheated with a bad product because I assume that the owners of the famous brand will want to protect the value of their famous brand. With wine perhaps we can't taste any difference but we assume that the prices reflect the judgment of oenologists who can. The famous brand with its high price serves to reduce risk when I feel incapable of judging quality.

> *Brands can reduce risk.*

Third, for some products the simple fact alone that the product is more expensive and that other people know that it is more expensive is valuable to me. I carry my Louis Vuitton bag, I wear my Rolex and my Armani, and everybody can see I am successful (assuming they don't think they are all fakes). In nature, animals allocate resources to having beautiful feathers, and so on, to signal their success and strength. In human society we do the same thing by buying luxury brands. As a result, just like animals in nature, we get better treatment from all around us because they respect us more. For example, when you step out of the back seat of your chauffeured Mercedes Benz wearing an expensive three-piece suit you get more respect from a police officer than if you step off your bicycle in dirty working clothes. The brand enhances you.

*Brands can get me respect.*

Fourth, for some products, perception creates reality. Meaning that if I drink a wine that I think is expensive it will taste better to me than if I think it is cheap. When I smell perfume that I think is expensive it smells better than if I think it is cheap. When I use medicine that I think is expensive it will work better than if I think it is cheap. In such cases, perception creates the reality. The brand creates the performance.[1]

Finally, some brands live on helping customers to deceive themselves with full consent from the customer. The premium water industry is the finest example of all. I understand there are even water sommeliers now. Kentwood water in Louisiana is drawn from a deep aquifer, the water is from rain that fell maybe 5,000 years ago, a thousand miles away on the Appalachian mountains, and has been filtered and mineralized ever since. People in Kentwood buy Kentwood water in the supermarket, even though they must know that the same water showers them in the morning and flushes the urinals at the local gas station.

They may be crazy but not as crazy as the people paying good money for Perrier water brought all the way from France to Los Angeles. "I prefer Perrier" they used to say. Must have been that whimsical teasing of the taste buds by the benzene. (Benzene was found in Perrier water in 1990 in the U.S. and then in Europe too.[2]) Brands are not a marketing trick to rip off irrational consumers ... unless that is what the customer wants.

*Brands help customers create a preferred reality.*

## How valuable is a brand?

Good products and good service create brands. Starbucks, Google, Amazon, Yahoo, iPod and so on, became new famous brands because of what they did, because of what they offered, not because they had brilliant brand strategies, but because they had brilliant new products and/or services.

> *Your product and your service make your brand famous.*

Provided your brand creates value for the customer, your brand can create value for your company. Interbrand, in cooperation with *Business Week*, annually releases its famous list of the world's most valuable brands. The ranking unfortunately appears to be based mostly on a company's profits; bravely ignoring that there could be other reasons than brand why some companies make a lot of money. To be fair, Interbrand makes its living doing brand consultancy so we can't blame them for attributing all earnings to a company's brand.[3]

Excellent profits can come from your strong brand, but also from a superior position achieved because everybody needs to use the software everybody uses, or because of technological prowess, or because of size, or because of great management, or because of great service, or because of great product design.

In 2006 Coca-Cola was, the world's most valuable brand, according to Interbrand.[4] That sounds reasonable. In any supermarket a two-liter bottle Coca-Cola can get as much as 50 cents more in price than a two-liter store-brand cola, even if consumers cannot taste any difference and there is no difference in production cost. The brand delivers value. It makes Coca-Cola taste better because it makes people think it tastes better. Also we look and feel better drinking a real Coke rather than a Sam Walton Coke. Fifty cents extra is a bargain.

But Microsoft is ranked the world's next most valuable brand. I'm surprised. Doesn't Interbrand know that people buy Word and PowerPoint, and so on, because it is a pain in the neck to use software different from what everybody else uses? In economic parlance, Microsoft has a natural monopoly due to network externalities. I wonder how much value the IRS brand has according to Interbrand calculations.

GE is the third most valuable brand. GE may be a great company, but do its huge earnings come from its brand? Maybe its refrigerator sales benefit from the GE brand, but for its major source of earnings, GE capital, I suspect that borrowers aren't so interested in the GE brand on the money they borrow. It's GE's scale and stellar credit that allows it to borrow at low rates and therefore offer financing on good terms to customers. It's GE's acknowledged managerial excellence and its prowess across a range of important technologies that ensures its competitiveness in many other businesses.

> *Brand is not the only possible source of excellent profits.*

Brand value can also be negative. I'm not sure if Interbrand has ever found any brands with negative brand value. But here is one example. General Motors in 2002 showed its new Pontiac Grand Am model to focus groups without informing these focus groups of the brand name for the new model. The car was put in competition with a number of competing Japanese and European models and it scored the best numbers GM had seen in its history: 60 percent of focus-group members said they liked the car the best among all alternatives. Unfortunately, when it was revealed that the car was a Pontiac, one third of the group didn't want it any more.[5] In other words, Pontiac must reduce price to maintain sales once it puts its name on a car. That is negative brand equity.

Hyundai has a problem too. In 2006 Hyundai beat Toyota and Honda according to J.D. Power's initial quality numbers. But consumers can't think of any reason to look at Hyundai. According to Hyundai's vice-president for sales David L Zuchowski: "When we don't have a price story, we have no story."[6] Hyundai's operating profit margin is 4.5 percent. Imagine how sweet it would be for Hyundai if it could add just 1 or 2 percent to its prices. Brand is not important to every company in every industry. But when brand is important, it is very expensive to have negative or zero brand equity.

> *When brand is important, poor brand equity is expensive.*

## Brand strategy

When brand strategy is important for a company's success, brand strategy must drive all four P and four C decisions. In turn those decisions should drive all other decisions such as HR, Finance, M&A, and so on.

When brand strategy is important, the company should *be* its brand. Put in the more beautiful words of Harvard Business School Professor John Deighton: "There is a vital interplay between the challenge a brand faces and the culture of the corporation that owns it."[7]

Deighton offers the example of Snapple, the funky brand built by a few friends who were basically expressing themselves through their business. After Quaker Oats bought Snapple, its managers immediately set out to destroy the brand. Quaker Oats turned Snapple into a non-cool company's idea of a cool brand. That's why Howard Stern, Rush Limbaugh, and the Snapple Lady, the visually, politically, socially incorrect threesome who had made the brand famous were quickly fired. Quaker Oats had been very successful with Gatorade. The company had great managerial talent, but it could not manage quirky Snapple, given its own cultural and systemic constraints. Any manager capable of even suggesting using Howard Stern as company spokesperson could never have existed inside Quaker Oats. Once Quaker Oats sold Snapple at a loss of more than $1 billion, the brand was just as quickly turned around again by private equity investor Triarc, its new owner. In their first week they not only rehired the Snapple lady. They put her picture on the bottle. The problem for Quaker Oats was that its culture simply did not allow managers to be funky and juvenile, no matter whether they all knew or not that that was what the brand needed.

Philips Electronics' recent "Sense and Simplicity" campaign is an example of a company trying to be its brand, to live its brand. The company discovered what everybody outside the consumer electronics industry already knows, namely, that consumers want sense and simplicity in technology. But rather than just presenting the slogan and encouraging simplicity in design, Philips decided to go a giant step further and become itself more sensible and simple. Instead of 500 businesses, there are now 70; instead of 30 divisions, there are now five. The more confusing parts of the company have been sold off. Internally, PowerPoint presentations can't have more than ten slides. "Be your brand" is Philips' strategy.[8]

> *When brand is important, you must be your brand.*

Will Philips' strategy work? It won't work until products and services by Philips are more sensible and simple than those by, say, Samsung and Sony. This will be easy. I mentioned Samsung before. Sony is worse. My Sony video camera came with one joint manual for three different models. On every page I have to figure out where the manual talks about my particular model.

When brand strategy is important, getting it right pays tremendous dividends. Not only will consumers be willing to pay more money for the same product, another key benefit of a competitive advantage based on a strong brand is that brand cannot be imitated.

Competitors can copy and improve on your product, offer a lower price, do much advertising, and give better service. But they are still not who you are. A Rolex copy watch may work better than the real thing, and maybe nobody can see it is a copy watch. But it still is a copy watch and even if nobody else knows, you know, and therefore you might buy one for fun, but you won't buy one to make yourself feel better about yourself. You won't buy one to wear every day.

The original Lexus was a copy Benz with the star missing. The car had to be sold at a very significant discount to the real thing. Someone driving a Lexus told the world two things: 1. I love Mercedes Benz; 2. I don't have the money. Better to buy an Audi then. It has taken a while for Lexus to develop its own identity.

Great products and great service build your brand. Then, when other companies copy everything you do, maybe even improve on what you do, then it's your brand's turn to protect you.

> *The brand says: "You can do what I can do. But you are not who I am."*

In the famous book *Blue Ocean Strategy*,[9] corporate strategy and brand strategy meet. One of the useful tools offered by the book allows companies to visually compare who they are relative to their direct and indirect competitors. Companies identify the relevant dimensions of their offerings (for car brands those might include price, safety, brand, speed, reliability, comfort, space) and then rank themselves relative to other players. The key to creating a "Blue Ocean Strategy" is to design an offering that does not follow the industry's existing patterns and tradeoffs of performance dimensions, but to instead create a different pattern of performance.

Thus, good brand strategy and good corporate strategy merge into one. A sound brand strategy offers direction to all company decisions, big and small, in a way that makes the company different from its industry, in a way that is internally consistent across the company's functions, in a way especially that will make it more difficult for different functions to beggar their neighbors, in a way to add value and differentiate the value offered by the company to its customers.

At Sony, I assume it's the logistics department that loves a single manual that serves different video cameras. The Sony marketing department suffers silently or maybe has never looked at the manual. In contrast, assuming Philips succeeds in living its promise, a marketing manager at Philips today will point to a manual that improves company convenience at the expense of consumer convenience and will say: "Sorry, that manual is not simple, it's not Philips."

> *Corporate strategy and brand strategy become one strategy.*

## The case of Intel

The most famous brand story of recent times is Intel. The company had to find a way to escape the commodity boom-and-bust nature of its business and the serious threat from Japanese and South Korean companies planning to take away its market. So, to simplify a long story, Intel bought a book about marketing and read the chapter on branding.[10]

I always say that nothing is more dangerous than an engineer with a marketing book since engineers have good habits that are a little harder to find among marketing managers. Engineers tend to be precise, they are careful, they read the whole book, and they like to measure things. Intel proves me right.

Intel came up with its famous campaign "Intel Inside." Remarkably, the personal computer companies, in exchange for discounts, collaborated in the process of their own commoditization, putting a rope around their necks by adding stickers to their computers saying "Intel Inside." Once the personal computer companies had put the rope around their necks, Intel pulled on the rope, as one does. When consumers went to the store and did not see the Intel Inside sticker we might expect the following conversation to ensue:

> *Consumer*: What's inside?
> *Store*: AMD.
> *Consumer*: Why not Intel?
> *Store*: It's the same, AMD is just as good.
> *Consumer*: If it's the same, why not Intel?
> *Store*: AMD is cheaper.
> *Consumer*: If it's cheaper, how is it the same? Anyway, I don't want to buy an expensive computer with a cheap chip inside.

That's the promise of the brand: you can do what I can do, but you are not who I am. AMD can make chips like Intel, but they are not Intel.

AMD can offer lower prices to the manufacturer, but the manufacturer has to lower the price of the computer when using AMD. Intel lets AMD live so Intel does not get into trouble with the antitrust authorities. When AMD gets too excited, Intel slaps AMD back down by dropping prices in whatever segments AMD tries to make its money.[11] Companies buying too many chips from AMD might also find it more difficult to get access to Intel's greatest and latest chips. According to the latest legal struggle between Intel and AMD that's how Intel was able to knock AMD back down in Japan, where its sales had been increasing more than Intel found acceptable. Intel, of course, denies any such thing and the Japanese companies prefer not to talk.[12]

Once engineers start reading a book they finish it. So Intel decided that perhaps two brands might be even better than one brand. Typical technical companies, for example Philips and Siemens, prefer to put the same brand on everything, from light bulbs to electric power plants. In contrast, Intel created a new brand: Celeron. Celeron is what I call a 'fighting' brand. Its purpose is not to make money. Its purpose is to fight with AMD. According to AMD, Intel does not make money on Celeron. The brand just exists to make life more difficult in AMD's market segments. Celeron is like Intel's dog. When AMD wants to fight, Intel refuses to fight and tells AMD: "Why don't you go fight with my dog Celeron." (The same rationale presumably drives major airlines to start up their own discount airlines.) Intel, of course, sees things differently, claiming that Celeron has been created as a new brand just to give customers more options.

> *Watch out for engineers who read marketing books.*

## ✍ POINTS TO REMEMBER

- ☞ **Brands can make decision-making easier.**
- ☞ **Brands can reduce risk.**
- ☞ **Brands can get me respect.**
- ☞ **Brands help customers create a preferred reality.**
- ☞ **Your product and your service make your brand famous.**
- ☞ **Brand is not the only possible source of excellent profits.**
- ☞ **When brand is important, poor brand equity is expensive.**

☞ **When brand is important, you must be your brand.**
☞ **The brand says: "You can do what I can do. But you are not who I am."**
☞ **Corporate strategy and brand strategy become one strategy.**
☞ **Watch out for engineers who read marketing books.**

## Notes

1. Various experiments on the relationship between what we think and what we experience can be found in *Proust Was a Neuroscientist* by Jonah Lehrer (Houghton Mifflin, 2007).
2. "When the Bubble Burst (Poor Management of Benzene Contamination Crisis by Perrier Group America Inc. and Source Perrier S.A.)," *The Economist (U.S.)* (August 1991). The Benzene is now removed. Presumably, the benzene accidentally contaminated the water during the process of adding carbon dioxide to the water to create the bubbles. Perrier admitted that the claim "naturally sparkling" had been a bit of an exaggeration.
3. For an explanation on how brand value is calculated by Interbrand see: "INNOVATION METRICS, The 100 Top Brands 2006, Here's How We Calculate the Power in a Name," http://bwnt.businessweek.com/brand/2006/
4. See http://www.interbrand.com
5. *Forbes* (9 December, 2002), p. 84.
6. David Kiley, "Hyundai Still Gets No Respect," *Business Week* (21 May 2007), pp. 68–70.
7. John Deighton, "How Snapple Got Its Juice Back," *Harvard Business Review* (January 2002), pp. 47–53.
8. Linda Tischler, "The Beauty of Simplicity," *Fast Company* (November 2005), p. 52.
9. W. Chan Kim and Renée Mauborgne, *Blue Ocean Strategy* (Harvard Business School Press, 2005).
10. Andy Grove, *Only the Paranoid Survive*, 1st edn (Currency, 1996).
11. Andy Reinhardt, "Intel is Taking No Prisoners," *Business Week* (12 July 1999), p. 38.
12. Roger Parloff, "Intel's Worst Nightmare," *Fortune* (21 August, 2006), p. 60.

# 14  Marketing Mathematics

## Key messages to whet your appetite

▶ Efficiency in marketing is easy but wrong
▶ Profit leads to market share
▶ High price is marketing's job
▶ Don't offer bonuses to mathematicians

## Mathematics

*Mathematics is not a favorite topic for marketing managers. Yet, it is an extremely important topic. In this chapter, more than in any other chapter, I will show how your common sense is not your friend. I am certain you will be very surprised at some of the assertions and results you will find in this chapter. You will be surprised to find that efficiency and profitability do not go together, you will be incredulous at the additional sales you will need to maintain profits when you lower your prices, you will understand the weakness of monetary incentives.*

## Efficiency is not the purpose

Colleagues always wonder about my teaching marketing mathematics in executive education, figuring it is the last thing managers want to listen to. But it has turned out to be among the most applauded pieces of teaching I do, especially among the most senior managers. So stick with me through this section. I promise it won't be unduly painful or complicated. Let us start with a case:

*Division manager Mr. Ratioman is not happy with sales manager Mr. Jansen. Mr. Ratioman has called Mr. Jansen into his office to demand an explanation for the disappointing performance of the subsidiary led by Mr. Jansen. His complaint is, "Mr. Jansen, one year ago you argued that you needed more salespeople. You had three, and you told me you could use three more. I gave you another three. This morning I examined your sales results over the past year. Sales expenses as a percentage of sales are up by almost 50 percent, sales per salesperson are down, and even sales per customer are down. We are spending more and getting less. Worse, I've also found out that your sales expenses as a percentage of sales are now the highest of all our divisions – other divisions have been able to lower their sales expenses while yours went up. You have been suggesting a promotion. Well, I suggest you go find work somewhere else."*

What do you say if you are Mr. Jansen? Do you apologize? Do you mumble something about fierce competition, the economy, the market? You should not. Instead, you should tell Mr. Ratioman that all the numbers he mentioned are irrelevant and all the changes in the numbers are the way they should be. You should tell Mr. Ratioman that you are surprised he is surprised.

Why are the numbers Mr. Ratioman mentions irrelevant? Because in marketing you must not try to be as efficient as possible: you should not try to have the lowest selling expenses or advertising expenses or whatever expenses per customer, per sales dollar, or per whatever. You should try only to maximize total profit – the pile of dollars you can take away from the game. And, as we will see, maximum profit and maximum efficiency can never be achieved at the same time. It is mathematically impossible.[1]

Nonetheless, many companies pursue the strange practice of sacrificing profits for (marketing) efficiency. Many companies, for example, evaluate sales managers not only on sales revenue and sales growth, but also on ratios such as sales per customer, sales per salesperson, selling expenses as a percentage of sales and so forth. These inappropriate measures encourage sales managers to steer away from maximizing profits in favor of optimizing pointless ratios.

To show how this is true I will run through the basic marketing mathematics numbers for a simple company.

*Firm A sells clothes. Its total fixed expenses for rent, electricity, wages equal $20,000 per month, plus it pays a fixed salary of $5,000 per month to one new outside salesperson. So total fixed expenses are $25,000 per month (fixed costs are costs a firm has regardless of sales). On average, the gross profit margin on the clothes sold by Firm A is equal to 25 percent (gross profit margin is the money as a percentage of sales left after paying for direct costs such as raw materials and/or parts, and so on; direct costs for Firm A are the cost of the clothes it sells). Aside from buying the clothes it sells and its fixed expenses,* *including the salesperson, Firm A has no other expenses. Firm A is a simple company, but essentially all companies are like this.*

**Question 1: What is the break-even level of sales for Firm A?**

**Answer 1: ($25,000÷0.25) = $100,000**

Fixed cost divided by gross profit margin gives the break-even level of sales, where you make neither a profit nor a loss.

**Question 2: Firm A currently has sales of $95,000. However, Firm A had sales of $60,000 before hiring the outside salesperson. Should Firm A keep the salesperson?**

**Answer 2: Yes.**

(Sales Revenue x Gross Margin) – Fixed Cost = Net Profit or Net Loss

With the salesperson, the company loses ($95,000 x 0.25) – $25,000 = – $1,250

Without the salesperson, the company loses ($60,000 x 0.25) – $20,000 = – $5,000

The salesperson helped Firm A cut losses from $5,000 to $1,250. How about hiring an additional salesperson?

**Question 3: Suppose Firm A hires another salesperson, paying the new salesperson also $5,000 per month. Again sales increase, but this time only by an additional $30,000, to a total of $125,000. Firm A is disappointed. Sales per salesperson are down significantly. Should Firm A get rid of the salesperson?**

**Answer 3: No.**

Firm A now makes ($125,000 x 0.25) – $30,000 = $1,250

The company finally makes a profit. But notice that salesperson expenses as a percentage of sales increased by almost 50 percent after the firm hired the new salesperson.

> **Without a salesperson, expenses were 0% (0 ÷ $60,000)**
> **With one salesperson, they were 5.26% ($5,000 ÷ $95,000)**
> **With two salespersons, they are 8% ($10,000 ÷ $125,000)**

Selling expenses clearly are completely out of control. Mr. Ratioman has some tough questions: "What is going on? What do you think you are doing? Don't you know the difficulties we face? Your numbers are the worst in the industry." Mr. Ratioman sounds convincing. And you would have one hell of a time finding a new job if you tell a prospective employer that you raised selling expenses as a percentage of sales by some 50 percent.

When companies face disappointing results, they invariably cut costs. (I never hear, "Upon hearing the disappointing results, CEO XYZ immediately ordered that the marketing budget be doubled.") The intuitive thinking is that poor results demand increased efficiency. And how do you become more efficient in the quickest possible way? You reduce spending. So how do you reduce spending? Do you reduce the cost of production? This is not so quick or easy to do. You cut advertising, you cut service, you cut sales expenditures, you cut promotion, you cut R&D. These are all areas where it is quick and easy to cut total costs and automatically become more efficient at the same time.

So suppose your boss tells you, "Go back to your office and cut costs. Do more with less." As a marketing manager, what do you say? You say, "No problem, boss!" Then take a look at your sales force. Suppose you have ten salespeople. Fire the one with the lowest sales. You cannot visit all customers any more? Not a problem. Choose a few smaller, more distant customers and tell them to take their business elsewhere. Now your sales per salesperson are up and your sales per customer are up. Your selling expenses as a percentage of sales are down. Your travel expenses as a percentage of sales are down too. Your total expenses are down also. Your remaining salespeople love you for making their jobs easier and their quota easier to achieve. Your 360-degree evaluations look great too. You are one great guy. (The guy you fired doesn't get to fill out an evaluation form.)You won't have any trouble finding a new job when you can show these numbers to a potential new employer.

> *Nothing is easier than achieving efficiency in marketing.*

Of course, not everything is perfect. Sales are down overall. But why blame this on you? Things are bad in the industry. Everybody knows that. That's why you had to cut costs. And you are showing yourself to be one tough manager, willing to make the hard choices, work harder and smarter, do less with more, and maintain team spirit to boot. What a guy. They call you Chainsaw Al.[2] And the company loses more money than ever before. Probably what the company needs is someone like you at the top.

This is not to say you should never cut back expenses. Business over time builds up fat. But the cutting away of fat should be an ongoing process. If you have been CEO for three years and then you respond to a loss with a major cost-cutting effort, I think the board of directors should ask what happened. Were you sleeping while you allowed unnecessary expenditures to accumulate? Or much worse, are you cutting costs in order to be seen doing something? Which costs exactly are you – or your managers – going to cut? It's all too easy to cut costs quickly and put yourself out of business slowly.

If inefficiency is not bad, exactly how inefficient should you get? Where is the limit? How do you calculate? For example, how many salespeople do you hire?

**Question 4: If Firm A hires yet another salesperson for $5,000 per month, by how much should sales go up (at a minimum) so Firm A is not worse off? (Put differently, what level of additional sales should Firm A achieve to break even on its salesperson expense of $5,000?)**

**Answer 4: $5,000 ÷ 0.25 = $20,000**

As long as additional salespeople bring in an extra $20,000, Firm A should keep hiring additional salespeople. More generally, here is a useful formula:

$$1 \div \text{Gross Profit Margin} = \text{Mandatory Marketing Leverage}$$

**In the case of Firm A, mandatory marketing leverage equals 1 ÷ 0.25 = 4**

This means that for any and all amounts Firm A spends on marketing, Firm A must get back four times that amount in additional sales. This mandatory marketing leverage (MML) number should be engraved in the mind of anyone in the company who is remotely related to marketing decision-making. This number is the touchstone for marketing decisions, for deciding on advertising budgets, for evaluating advertising and promotion experiments, for deciding on the size of the sales force – in short, for any investment in marketing.

> *Mandatory marketing leverage is the touchstone for marketing spending decisions.*

Order your marketing managers to think of as many ways as possible of spending more money, provided that any amount of additional money they spend brings in, at a minimum, four times (in the case of Firm A) that amount in additional sales. This is hard work for the marketing managers – much harder than cutting costs and becoming more efficient. They have to get creative and they have to measure their results (always a good idea). While measuring the effectiveness of advertising has generally not been a favorite pastime, new cost consciousness and new technology are putting an end to those good old days.

In particular the current joint venture "Project Apollo" between Arbitron and Nielsen, using portable people meters to measure exposure to ads plus home scanners to keep track of purchases, promises to enable advertisers to measure the relationship between advertising exposure and purchase behavior more accurately than ever before. What happens when sales increase too much, straining your capacity? You might have to increase prices a little, say 1 percent. How much does net profit increase when you raise price by 1 percent? On average, across industries, when firms are able to raise price by 1 percent, they increase net profit by 11.3 percent.[3] Are you surprised that 1 percent difference in price makes such a great difference to net profit? Consider the case in the next section.

## Marketing's job is to increase the price we can get

*Division manager Mr. Ratioman also is not happy with marketing manager Mr. Zhang. He has called Mr. Zhang into his office. "Mr. Zhang," he says, "you decided six months ago to raise our prices by 10 percent. I let you do it. Now, six months later, our sales are down by 15 percent. It doesn't take a genius to figure out that, even with the price increase, we are now taking in less money than before. Obviously, our demand is price-elastic (disproportionately sensitive to price), and I would have thought you might have tried to determine price elasticity before you decided to increase our prices."*

What would you say if you were Mr. Zhang? Most managers I work with have surprisingly poor intuition on changes in price and consequent changes in sales that will be acceptable (maintain profit) or not. Surprisingly, marketing textbooks have no simple formula to calculate how much sales need to go up or down to compensate for a price decrease or price increase. Most marketing textbooks talk about price elasticity, implicitly creating the impression that when demand is price-elastic it is a good idea to lower your price because the demand increase will outweigh the price decrease. Conversely, when demand is price-inelastic you should raise price. If this makes intuitive sense to you, then intuition is not your friend and you should pay close attention to the following. First, since marketing does not have a simple formula to help you make the right decisions I have created one.

**Dividing old gross profit margin by new gross profit margin gives you the percentage of sales that new sales in dollars must be (at a minimum) of old sales in dollars.**

or

**Minimum New Sales Revenue = (Old Gross Profit Margin/ New Gross Profit Margin) * Old Sales Revenue**

For example:

**Question 5: Suppose Firm A raises its prices by 10 percent, and sales (in dollars) go down by 15 percent. Should Firm A keep its higher prices, or should it lower prices back down?**

**Answer 5: Firm A should keep its higher prices.**

**Old gross margin was 25 percent. So a dress selling for $100 costs Firm A $75. Now that dress sells for $110, so the new gross profit will be $35 on a sale of $110. The new gross profit margin will be $35 ÷ $110 = 0.318. Applying the formula yields: 0.25÷0.318 =0.786 (78.6%).**

This means that after Firm A increased price by 10 percent, Firm A will be better off as long as Firm A's new sales revenue is at least 0.786 (78.6 percent) of old sales revenue. Since sales went down by 15 percent, Firm A will be better off than before.

**Old situation: 0.25 x $125,000 = $31,250**
**New situation: (new margin) 0.318 x (new sales of) 0.85 x $125,000 = $33,787.50**

But what about fixed costs? This is a question I frequently get when I show this result. Are not fixed costs higher now? No, fixed costs are fixed. They were $30,000. With production down by 15 percent, they will still be $30,000. So are fixed costs not higher now per unit? Yes, they are. And why do you care? Don't divide. Get out of the ratio habit. What matters is total gross profit and total net profit, not cost per unit or per window in your office, or whatever. Since gross profit increased from $31,250 to

$33,787.50, and fixed costs are fixed, net profit increased from $1,250 to $3,787.50. Not bad. Even better, you just freed up 15 percent of capacity in your factories that you can now use for something else.

A similar formula works also for calculating minimum new sales in units.

**Dividing old gross profit per unit by new gross profit per unit gives you the percentage of sales in units that new sales must be (at a minimum) of old sales in units.**

or

**Minimum New Sales in Units =**
**(Old Gross Profit per Unit/New Gross Profit per Unit)\*Old Sales in Units**

**Question 6: Suppose Firm A sells suits for a price of $500 and its gross profit is still 25 percent, so Firm A purchases these suits for $375. Now suppose Firm A raises its price from $500 to $550 for a suit. How many sales of suits and how many customers can Firm A afford to lose to keep the same profit it was making before?**

**Answer 6: Up to 28.6 percent of sales in units.**

**The old gross profit per unit was $125, and new gross profit per unit is $175. Therefore, in units Firm A only needs to maintain 125÷175 = 71.4 percent of old sales to keep the same profit as before the price increase. Thus it can afford to lose up to 28.6 percent of its sales of suits when it increases prices by 10 percent.**

If you are surprised at this result, you are not the only one. This suggests to me that many price discussions and recommendations, if they are taken on gut feeling, will be far from optimal for the firm. One difference between MBA students, compared to more seasoned managers, is that MBAs are quicker to recommend lowering price and increasing advertising as a cure-all for low sales. Their recommendations suggest that sales maximization is their intuitive goal for the firm. Experienced managers also suffer from this bias, but less severely so.

Since lowering price is so popular, let us calculate what happens when we lower price.

**Question 7: Suppose Firm A lowers its prices by 10 percent. How much should sales go up, at a minimum, to make up for the lower price (so profit stays the same)?**

**Answer 7:** Old gross profit margin/new gross profit margin = 0.25 ÷ 0.166 = 1.506

Old gross profit per unit/new gross profit per unit = $25 ÷ $15 = 1.67

**The piece of clothing that sold for $100 now sells for $90. The gross profit per unit has gone from $25 to $15. So our gross margin has changed from 25 percent to 16.6 percent ($15 ÷ $90). Thus sales must go up by a bit over 50 percent (0.25 ÷ 0.166) in dollars in order to make up for the 10 percent decrease in price, and they have to go up by an astounding 67 percent (15 ÷ 25) in units.**

> *Lowering price is the most expensive marketing strategy of all.*

Managers are invariably surprised by –and a few simply disbelieve – these results. Faced with a choice between intuition and mathematics, however, we have to go with the mathematics. Intuition is not always our best friend. Notice that if sales have to go up by 67 percent, fixed costs probably are no longer fixed. You may have to build another factory.

There is a fundamental point here. The job of marketing is not just to sell a product. Anyone can sell a product as long as the price is low enough. *The job of marketing is to find and keep great customers so we can sell a product at a good price.* This is why we differentiate the product, segment the market, offer added services and so forth. In short, this is why we do marketing – *to escape price as a tool for competition.* Keeping costs low is the job of production. Keeping prices high is the job of marketing.

> *Keeping costs low is the job of production. Keeping prices high is the job of marketing.*

The market may force you at times to lower your price. But a lower price will rarely make you rich. Lower price, as opposed to lower cost, is not a sign of strength. (Wal-Mart is an exception. Lower prices are its competitive advantage. In marketing there are always exceptions.) But, typically, lower price is a sign of competitive weakness, a lack of imagination, a lack of customer loyalty, a lack of safe customer relationships.

What about market share? Isn't that important? Managers always ask this question. My answer always is: absolutely! Market share is key to long-term survival, especially in a world of global consolidation in so many industries. But this is exactly why you need to focus on profit. If you achieve high returns on investment, the whole world will rush to put its money into your pockets. Stock exchanges will compete to list your company. Shareholders will compete for shares in your IPO. Companies with profit can always buy companies with market share.

> *Profit comes before market share and leads to market share.*

We should look at profit not merely as the result of what we do, the output of our actions of yesterday, but also as input, providing the tools or weapons we need for tomorrow's game – to defend ourselves – or to conquer. Poor companies cannot protect their markets, their technological edge, or themselves.

I know the conventional wisdom: Think long term, keep prices low, maximize market share. Japanese companies always received much admiration for their long-term thinking. Journalists believe this sort of stuff, ever repeating that trite phrase, "Wall Street's obsession with quarterly profits."[4] But you shouldn't believe this. Short-term profit is just what the doctor ordered. It gets you to long-term profit. I am talking about real profits here, not about profits manufactured by the accounting department or profits achieved by cheating customers with bad service.

> *There is nothing wrong with short-term profit; it gets you to long-term profit.*

## Don't use bonuses to motivate mathematicians

*Sales manager Jansen is very happy with Dan Padgett, the new salesman he has hired to prepare a complex technical bid for $2,000,000 in new business. Padgett is an excellent electrical engineer with an undergraduate degree in mathematics. Jansen has offered the new salesman a $40,000 bonus on top of his regular salary if the company wins the bid. Jansen had argued hard for this big bonus, explaining to his company that technical salespeople like Padgett are basically hired guns who will move from one company to the other as they please, always in search of the best payoff. Jansen estimates that if Padgett does not work hard on the bid there is a 30 percent chance of* *winning the bid. If Padgett works hard there is a 40 percent chance of winning the bid. It's definitely worth it to the company to offer Padgett the big bonus. Padgett honestly told Jansen that he would like to earn $10,000 more for working hard on this bid compared to not working hard. Will Padgett work hard on this bid? What bonus should we offer Padgett to make sure he will work hard? Is $40,000 enough?*

When people decide to work hard or not work hard, the first thing they do is figure out whether hard work makes any significant difference to the results. Padgett, of course, is very much qualified to calculate the right commission that would justify his working hard. What difference does it make to him if he works hard or not? Let's see:

Winning the bid gets Padgett a $40,000 commission:

If he does not work hard he has a 30 percent chance of getting a $40,000 bonus. A 30 percent chance of $40,000 is equal to $12,000.

If he does work hard he improves his chance of success to 40 percent. A 40 percent chance of $40,000 is equal to $16,000.

The difference between 12,000 and 16,000 is far from enough to motivate Padgett to work hard. He told Jansen he needed to see a difference of $10,000 to work hard. A difference of $4,000 is not big enough. The bonus of $40,000 needs to be increased to $100,000 before Padgett gets motivated to work hard. Unfortunately, a bonus of $100,000 may be too much for the company to stomach.

The lesson from this calculation is that people do not work hard in order to earn a salary and build a career. People work hard for the difference that working hard makes in their salary and career. Especially in marketing, working hard is only one factor in people's success, the company's products and prices, competitors' actions, changes in the economy, dumb luck, and so on, are also factors.

Since success depends on a variety of factors, working hard or not may not make all that much difference to the income our salesman gets. Many salespeople and marketing managers intuitively calculate that working really hard to get a raise or bonus is not worthwhile (making their company *think* that they work hard can still be worthwhile though).

*What is the difference to your salespeople and marketing managers whether they work hard or not?*

## ✍ POINTS TO REMEMBER

☞ Nothing is easier than achieving efficiency in marketing.

☞ Mandatory marketing leverage is the touchstone for marketing spending decisions.

☞ Lowering price is the most expensive marketing strategy of all.

☞ Keeping costs low is the job of production. Keeping prices high is the job of marketing.

☞ Profit comes before market share and leads to market share.

☞ There is nothing wrong with short-term profit; it gets you to long-term profit.

☞ What is the difference to your salespeople and marketing managers whether they work hard or not?

## Notes

1. Except in theory in the special case where profit is exactly zero, but it is not productive to worry about that here.
2. Al Dunlap gained fame by destroying Scott Paper and Sunbeam by way of cost cutting. Until reality caught up with him, he was very proud of his efforts, as he describes in his book, *Mean Business: How I Save Bad Companies and Make Good Companies Great* (Fireside, 1997).
3. According to an analysis of P&L statements for 2,463 companies in the Compustat database, as reported by M.V. Marn and R.L. Rosiello, in their article "Managing Price, Gaining Profit," *Harvard Business Review* (September/October 1992).
4. The Internet stock market bubble of 2000 suggests Wall Street, or at least investors, need a bigger obsession with quarterly profits.

# 15  Pricing Strategies

> ## Key messages to whet your appetite
>
> ▶ There is more to price than just price
> ▶ Price is the last P
> ▶ Price discrimination is where the money is
> ▶ It's hard to pay too much attention to pricing

## You can't know too much about pricing

*I argued in the previous chapter that it is the factory's job to make costs low, and it is marketing's job to make prices high. In this chapter I describe some of the strategies your marketing managers can use to make prices higher, preferably without your customers noticing. Fortunately, for marketing managers, people are not mathematicians and thus there are many ways we can make people both poorer and happier or at least not unhappier. Are these strategies ethical and honest? Some are and some are not. Sellers have a right to try to get a better price just like buyers have a right to get a lower price. But remember to be wary of strategies that produce a sale at a higher price at the expense of an unhappy customer. Here are some of the things we know and use in marketing.*

## Percentages and numbers are two different things

An experiment showed that 59 percent of psychiatrists will release a mental patient if they are informed that "20 out of every 100 [similar] patients" likely will commit an act of violence within six months after release. But when they are told that "similar patients have a 20 percent chance" of committing an act of violence, no fewer than 79 percent will release the patient.[1] Aside from implications for public safety, it is very interesting how supposedly professional judgment is significantly affected by simple differences in methods of presentation. Percentages are not people. Only people are people. That's why 20 people out of 100 is more than 20 percent.

If you want people to think a number is big, talk about the number not about the percentage. If you want people to think a number is small, talk about the percentage. Car companies offer a "$2,000 cash back discount" to customers willing to buy before the end of the month. $2,000 cash back sounds like a lot more than an 8 percent discount on a $25,000 car.

In contrast, Wall Street financial wizard fund managers charge a mere 1.9 percent or so in "expenses" annually, calculated as a percentage of funds invested. That sounds confusing but it doesn't sound like much money. Besides these are "expenses" aren't they? It is only fair that you pay for expenses, especially when these expenses are a mere 1.9 percent.

But the result is that an investor with a $500,000 301K pays his fund managers $10,000 annually in fees. Suppose he earns a salary of $90,000 and keeps $60,000 net. That means he is working full time for two months each year to have someone move his money from GE to Home Depot and back again in his 301K. People worry about how much they pay in tax to the government. Meanwhile, investors pay a huge "advice tax" to the financial industry and they don't complain and probably don't even know how much they pay. The financial industry has done a fantastic pricing job.

> *Use numbers for discounts. Talk percentages for charges.*

## The power of three

McDonald's has three sizes of French fries and milk shakes. Many restaurants offer set menus for lunch at three different price levels. Looking closely at shirts for sale in stores you might notice three price "lines." What is so special about having three options?

Here is what is so special. If I offer two sizes of cappuccino, one Grande for $2.69 cents and one Tall Grande for $3.29 cents, then maybe half the people buy Grande and half buy Tall Grande. If I add a third option of Super Grande for $4.29 maybe nobody buys that Super Grande, but now only 20 percent buy Grande and 80 percent buys Tall Grande. Thus the purpose of the third option is to get customers to buy the second option. Meanwhile, outside the store we have a huge sign saying: Cappuccino Grande for only $2.69!

According to Dave Thomas, when he introduced a triple burger at Wendy's, some managers opposed the idea arguing that nobody had a mouth big enough for a triple burger. Dave Thomas agreed that the triple burger was not a hit, but he pointed out that as a result Wendy's did start selling a lot of double burgers.[2]

## Start from the top

Street vendors around the world like to start negotiations with a totally exorbitant price. The smart customer smiles and offers a price that is maybe a third of the obviously ridiculous price. Much haggling ensues and finally a price of a bit more than a third of the originally quoted price is settled on. Everybody is happy. You even feel a bit guilty. But you'll get over that guilt feeling pretty quickly once you discover your new acquisition for sale in a nearby department store for less than half of what you paid.

Similarly, Robert Cialdini[3] reports on an experiment where customers shopping for a pool table who were first shown a $3,000 pool table spent more than $1,000. Customers who were first shown lower priced tables and then were encouraged to buy a more expensive table ended up buying on average a table for $550.

In psychology this effect is called "anchoring." While the $3,000 price may be far outside what the customer wants to spend; it does adjust upward what he will, in fact, spend. Antiques stores will put a few pieces for sale with totally ridiculous prices. Customers will look at these overpriced high-priced items, scoff at the idea that any fool would pay so much, and then happily spend on something else twice more than what they were planning to spend.

Simply throwing around big numbers already helps. If you want to sell a house for $500,000, you should say "1 million" a few times. For example, you can say "There are about 1 million people in the larger metro area" or "Many houses this size will sell for more than a million in most other cities" or "I have told my husband a million times to put the dishes in the sink."

## Talk value

It is not always easy to perceive a product's value. Remember that your customers are rarely expert on the value of the product you sell them. You must be the expert. So what is value? What determines value? Philosophers have thought about this question for many thousands of years already. The Greeks wondered why it is that water is more precious than gold, but gold has the higher price.

You probably own a TV. Do you know its value? Here is how I present the problem to my students. Imagine that you can buy a new 48 inch plasma TV, either Sony-branded or K-Mart. Both TVs are made by the same company in China. The Sony costs you $5,000. The K-Mart costs $4,000. Looking at the issue from a purely financial perspective, which TV should you buy?

K-Mart TV seems the better choice. But suppose you bought an apartment for some $300,000. In that apartment the living room is the most important room, the square yard or so of floor or wall space holding the TV is the most central square yard in the living room (even when the TV is off, we still look at the TV), the two square inches announcing the brand, Sony or K-Mart, are the most central square inches on the TV. Your TV brand name is the center of the center of the center of what may be your most valuable asset.

Is it wise to put the K-Mart brand at this very center of your greatest investment? What do you think will happen when you get ready to sell your apartment? You may discover that everybody in your building gets the price they ask, but your apartment is just not moving. Why? Maybe people subconsciously use the cheap brand of TV you have on the wall as a cue to form an opinion on whether or not your art on the wall comes from a gallery or from your children, whether the wood floor is expensive or cheap, whether your doors are plastic or wood underneath the paint, whether the kitchen cabinets are solid wood or K-Mart specials and so on. That could be one very expensive K-Mart TV you bought. (I'm not knocking K-Mart here or Wal-Mart. Buy your clothes, your furniture, your art, your plants, your kitchen cabinets, everything, from K-Mart or Wal-Mart. Then put the biggest, most expensive brand plasma TV you can find on the wall and all will be well.)

*R&D value and talk value.*

## Don't talk price

Once I was working my way through a narrow alley in Hong Kong filled with vendors offering clothes, leather purses, copy watches, souvenirs, and what not. Forget about a relaxed stroll taking in the sights. Everybody wants to sell you everything. One man in particular followed me persistently, shouting "Only 20 Hong Kong dollars, only 20 Hong Kong dollars!"

What was he selling? I have no idea and I will never know. That man broke an important rule of marketing. Price is the last P in marketing, not the first P. Good marketing stays away from mentioning the price of a product as long as possible. Price is a negative in your relationship with the customer.

The Rainbow vacuum company in the United States knows this rule.[4] The company manages to sell its vacuum cleaners at a price of around $1,000. They sell these vacuum cleaners door to door. Their potential customers already have vacuum cleaners. Vacuum cleaners should only cost $50 to maybe $300. How can Rainbow possibly sell to anybody?

The product does have a unique difference: the dirt does not go into a paper bag. The air is vacuumed through a container with water, and the water captures the dirt. After vacuuming, the dirty water is disposed off. Presumably this way you catch more dirt. The salespeople demonstrate how the air leaving a regular vacuum cleaner still holds a lot of dirt. This dirt will hang in the air, affecting your lungs, aggravating breathing problems, worsening asthma, giving you allergies and whatnot.

Interested customers naturally inquire about the price. Salespeople know that the sales conversation will finish when they mention price. "I don't want to tell you the price," they respond, "I don't want you to buy this product because of the price, but because you really need it." They offer a dramatic demonstration of how a pillow can be put in a plastic bag and sucked to a very small hard shape with the Rainbow vacuum cleaner.

Customers may again ask about the price. The salespeople will respond that if they and the customer together decide that the customer does need this vacuum cleaner that they personally will make sure the customer can buy one. The salespeople demonstrate the full value of the product, the money saved on not having to buy paper bags for the vacuum cleaner, the money saved in doctors' prescriptions, the money saved in days not taken off work, the money saved in not having to replace carpets that wear out sooner when regular vacuum cleaners leave grinding dirt behind. So much in savings that customers may wonder why the government does not make these vacuum cleaners mandatory. Only after some two or three hours, after the customer practically begs on his knees for the price, will the price be revealed.

You might think it is impossible to sell a vacuum cleaner for $1,000 or more to people who already have a vacuum cleaner? Think again. If the salesperson crosses the threshold, a sale results one out of three times.

Beauty is in the eye of the beholder and so is value. And it won't be in the eye of the beholder if you don't put it there. So be an expert on the value of your product. Do R&D on the value of your product. Then invest to put that value in the eye, the mind, of the customer, then talk price. Then the seemingly impossible becomes possible.

> *Talk value. Don't talk price.*

You might wonder how you can avoid mentioning price. One way to accomplish this as we just saw is to simply refuse to talk price until the discussion about value is complete. Another way is to start with an outrageously high price like the street vendor does. Yet another way is to start with an outrageously low price. Can this get you a better price in the end?

It might not just get you a better price. It might get you a sale where you got none before. John Stack of A City Discount sells restaurant equipment on eBay. He started out by listing his items at prices he was willing to accept. Unfortunately, no one bid. So he changed tactics and listed items at one dollar. That's like not giving a price at all. So what was the result?

An industrial ice-cream maker first listed for $999 had failed to attract a single bid. Then Stack listed it for $1. This time the ice cream maker drew bids and sold for $2,000. Ongoing experimentation confirmed this was not a fluke. Now he prices 95 percent of all used equipment at a price of $1. He started on eBay in 1999, closed his old store in 2001, and reached a sales level by 2003 that exceeded by ten times his sales of 1998. An excellent success and, even better, he has one less thing to worry about now that customers set the prices.[5]

According to Stack, "When you start something at a dollar, it seems people bid on it and develop an attachment to it, even if they have to go above what they originally intended." No doubt this emotional aspect is part of the story. Also, the act of bidding itself becomes an investment. If we stop bidding we lose that investment and you already know how much we hate to lose.

But I also believe that the following is true and important: when we show the equipment with a price of $999 customers think about the price; when we show the equipment with a price of $1 customers think about the equipment. Price is a negative and, if at all possible, should come at the end of our story to the customer, not at the beginning.

> *Price is never the first P.*

## Price cues

Customers know roughly what things should cost, but only roughly. There is but little time and there are too many products. That's why customers use price cues to decide if something is priced right.

There are high price cues: deep leather couches, thick carpet, dark wood, burgundy, crystal, deep voices from three-piece suits. Mercedes Benz has leather couches in the showroom and won't have a Presidents' Day Sale. An expensive clothing store might offer you a glass of wine. A friend once volunteered to pay for a round of cognac and randomly selected from several brands suggested by the waiter. Then we (minus our friend) had the pleasure of being introduced to a really impressive high price cue: a big book bound in leather kept in a nice cherry wood box for him to sign. Everybody who orders this cognac gets to sign the book, the waiter explained.

Low price cues include fluorescent lighting, sale signs, cheap flooring, workers who are not too attractive, dressed in cheap smocks. Note that high price cues don't necessarily cost more than low price cues. A smock can be done in a nice burgundy or it can be done in K-Mart blue light special. The cost is the same, but the message is different.

One common low price cue is the nine price ending. Because customers use cues, it is perfectly possible for sales to increase when a price is increased from say $34 to $39.[6]

When a price ends on a nine the seller implicitly communicates that the item is priced carefully. The difference between $9.99 and $10.00 is minuscule. But the difference in the implied message matters. When a price ends on a '0' the customer suspects the price has been rounded up and that the seller doesn't worry about the price. Monopoly prices and punishment prices end on a zero, like laundry in a hotel, a parking ticket, an IRS late filing penalty.

Of course, there are shady sellers who combine high prices with low price cues. Not just rent-to-own outlets but also banks offering credit cards with an initial AMAZING! rate of 6.99 percent, which later silently goes to 18.99 percent. But because sellers with low prices generally use low price cues and sellers with high prices do not, rational consumers do rely on price cues because it makes sense to rely on them

> *Low price cues work for sellers because they work for buyers.*

There are also sellers who combine low prices with high price cues. This works well if the high price cues add value to the customer experience and if you count on repeat business and word of mouth to build your company. Zea Rotisserie & Grill and Semolinas are two examples of restaurant chains trying to look expensive while charging very average prices.

So if you want to increase sales, you can reduce price further (the most expensive thing you can do as you know). Or perhaps you could increase high price cues: buy a statue, buy a chandelier with candles (burn the candles halfway down, then don't light them any more), and so on. If you repair appliances, maybe you should invest in a nice uniform and a clean toolbox. If you are a Hyundai dealer, have the nicest waiting room, better than Mercedes Benz, for customers who get their car repaired. Have a television, current magazines, fresh coffee, fruit juice, and wifi. Make the minuscule investment in high price cues. Customers will be pleasantly shocked when they see your actual price. You will be one of those "best-kept secrets" of your town.

Earlier I characterized Wal-Mart and K-Mart as discount stores for middle-class and poor people, respectively. The products and prices in the two stores may not be so different. But compared to Wal-Mart, it appears K-Mart has more emphatic low price cues. Wal-Mart offers low prices with average price cues.

*Be cheap. Look nice. Maybe that can work for you.*

## Price endings

While the nine price ending dominates in Western countries, in many East Asian countries eight price endings are also very common. More than 40 percent of prices on restaurant menus in Hong Kong end with an eight. The eight isn't a cue for price but a cue for quality. The number eight stands for prosperity and good fortune. In an experiment I performed in China, with a sample of 1,250 women, I found that substantial percentages of women found prices more acceptable when they ended on a five, or eight, or nine. The worst price ending proved to be one. For example for a particular pharmaceutical product, experiments showed that 62 percent of women were willing to pay 31 cents, while 73 percent were willing to pay 35 cents. Possibly, a five price ending works for consumers who round up or down when looking at prices.[7]

A one price ending is very unkind. $10.01? That extra penny feels like a fine, like a tax. The opposite should hold true for quantities. Don't sell an 11.9 oz. bottle of shampoo. Sell a 12.1 oz. bottle.

*Nine is fine, a five is nice too, and an eight can be nice in Asia.*

## Sale anyone?

A sign on a store item that says "Sale" can increase sales by 50 percent even if the price is unchanged.[8] Shoppers may appear irrational, but most of the time, in most stores, when a sign says "Sale" the price is, in fact, lower than what it normally is. Customers rationally assume that even if they don't know what the price really should be, that some other customers probably do know, and that therefore the store will not increase the price for an item above the regular price and then post a "Sale" sign. Shoppers in grocery stores are mostly right about this. But when consumers buy products where hardly anyone knows what the price should be, say furniture, the opportunity exists to charge higher prices with a bigger "Sale" sign.

The impact of a "Sale" sign on sales moreover is not merely due to customers' perception that the value is now better; another simple reason for the increased sales is that any item with a sign on it draws more attention. Balloons can work just as well. I did an experiment for a chain of daiquiri stores. While the prices charged to customers for different daiquiris such as White Russian, Jungle Juice, and what have you, are all the same, the costs and margins for the store are quite different. So I advised tying balloons to the dispensers of the highest-margin options and, no surprise there, sales for those items went up.

Restaurants similarly might offer their highest-margin items as "Today's Specials" with a discount. But they can also draw little balloons next to the higher-margin items in the menu, claiming that the item is "Our cook's favorite," leaving unsaid whether it's the cook's favorite because it tastes the best, or is easiest to cook, or because the cook is paid based on gross margins.

Don't use too many sales signs though. An experiment in a Chicago supermarket with frozen fruit juice showed that putting sale signs on more than 30 percent of items decreased total sales in the category.[9] When there are too many sale signs the message taken away by the customer is that the 'on sale' prices cannot be trusted and therefore the regular prices also cannot be trusted.

## Price discrimination

The price to fly one way on United Airlines from Amsterdam to New Orleans on 20 July 2007 equaled $2,703; the price to take the same flight on United, plus take a return flight three weeks later from New Orleans back to Amsterdam equaled less than half that price, only $1,184. See here the beauty and madness of price discrimination. Business people take one-way flights. Tourists buy round trips.

Of course, you can try to be a smart guy. Once, when I had to fly one way from Amsterdam to Shanghai, I purchased a return ticket to save money. I learned an important lesson. Don't be a smart guy. When I gave the ticket for reimbursement to the finance office at my university I was told, "No. Sorry. EU regulations require that you first finish the trip before you are reimbursed." Live and learn.

> *Don't be a smart guy.*

Demand curves show the relationship between your price and the quantity you can sell. Each point on the demand curve represents some individual who decides that at that price point they still buy. But if the price goes up by 1 cent, that particular individual decides not to buy. The value of that product to that customer no longer exceeds its price. Ideally we charge each person exactly that price where they just still buy.

Companies normally can't get to that ideal, but J.D. Byrider Systems, Inc., may have found a way. The company sells used cars to people with marginal credit. Rather than putting a price on the cars, salespeople ask detailed questions about the customers' financial situation and then use proprietary software to set the down payment, interest rate, payments, and total price: pure value-based pricing, charging what the market can bear. According to Byrider, fewer than 10 percent of its customers ask about the price of the car. Consumer activists are not pleased, especially since interest rates on the car loans run as high as 24.9 percent (but not 25.1 percent).[10]

> *The right price is different for different customers.*

More typically, companies try to get closer to the ideal by separating customers in groups that attach greater or lesser value to the product or who have less or more options and/or incentive to go somewhere else. Companies segment by price sensitivity.

For example, companies kindly offer special discounts to grandma and grandpa and to students. Actually, most elderly consumers in the U.S. have more money to spend than 30-something couples with a mortgage, two car loans, student loans, credit cards, and two or three children. But older customers have more time to shop around and that is why companies offer discounts to the elderly, be they rich or poor. Students too have more time to shop, plus they have less money. Discounts to old people and to students are the natural outcome of a pricing policy that tries to charge everybody as much as possible.

Discounts to the elderly or to students are straightforward. Much more subtle tools for price discrimination can be found. My recent favorite tool is "empathy with the poor" as described in the excellent book *The Undercover Economist*.[11] The author, Tim Harford, tells the story of Costa Coffee, a coffee shop in London which offered its customers the option to pay 20 cents extra for coffee brewed with "Fair Trade" coffee. Fair Trade coffee is purchased at a premium of about $1 per pound from poor coffee farmers adding about 2 cents to the shop's cost of a cup of coffee. The store took 90 percent of the money intended for the coffee farmer.

Apparently for the shop it was not enough to rob the farmers; it was felt a good idea also to rob those who feel bad about farmers being robbed. Costa Coffee engaged in price discrimination, using 'fair trade' as a means to charge different prices to different customers.

Actually nobody robs the farmers. They are victims of unfavorable terms of trade for undifferentiated commodities with very elastic supply. Robbery is the right word though for taking 90 percent of the money well-intentioned people contribute to help coffee farmers. When Harford inquired with Costa Coffee about the small percentage of the fair trade charge that would find its way to the farmers, the company decided to stop its practice and offer fair trade coffee on request without charging anything extra.

Can you raise the price for some segment of your customers, and lower the price for some other segment? Can you create differentiation between your low-priced and high-priced options? You can differentiate based on time of consumption (lower prices for the early show or for flights on Saturday), based on ordering conditions (lower prices when you buy over the Internet or when you order three weeks in advance), based on choices (have five options at high prices and one option at a low price), based on place of purchase (higher price for a beer on the terrace with the great view, lower for a beer inside), based on sensitivity to the difficult life of poor coffee farmers (Costa Coffee), and so on. Your engineers invent new products. Your marketing managers should invent new tools for price discrimination.

*Use creativity, new inventions, R&D to find new ways of price discrimination.*

But be careful. Unless you are a monopolist, do not artificially reduce the quality of your lower-priced alternatives. IBM once created the PC Jr., which offered much less computer for the lower price. Given that other companies already were offering much more computer for the same lower prices, all IBM accomplished was to make its competitors look better in the eyes of consumers shopping at the lower-price points. In another example of misguided quality deterioration purely for the purpose of price discrimination, the Ramada in Paris put me in a cheap room first and then upgraded me to a more expensive room. I didn't see any difference until I noticed that the cheap room didn't offer some minor amenities such as a $20 coffee machine or a $10 hair dryer. That sort of game-playing builds opportunity for "low prices but high price cues" competitors.

## Conclusion

Given that companies on average increase profits by 11.3 percent if they increase prices by a mere 1 percent it seems you can hardly spend too much attention on your pricing strategies. Pricing does not get the attention and respect it deserves compared to the attention paid to promotion and branding. Companies use advertising agencies and PR agencies, and so on, but not pricing agencies. They should. Many companies could use the help. One thing should be abundantly clear, prices are not just numbers and people are not natural mathematicians. You should expect and achieve the same creativity in your pricing strategies that you look for in your other strategies.

---

*It's hard to pay too much attention to pricing.*

---

✎ **POINTS TO REMEMBER**

☞ Use numbers for discounts. Talk percentages for charges.
☞ R&D value and talk value.
☞ Talk value. Don't talk price.
☞ Price is never the first P.

- ☞ **Low price cues work for sellers because they work for buyers.**
- ☞ **Be cheap. Look nice. Maybe that can work for you.**
- ☞ **Nine is fine, a five is nice too, and an eight can be nice in Asia.**
- ☞ **Don't be a smart guy.**
- ☞ **The right price is different for different customers.**
- ☞ **Use creativity, new inventions, R&D to find new ways of price discrimination.**
- ☞ **It's hard to pay too much attention to pricing.**

## Notes

1. These findings are reported by Sarah Lichtenstein and Paul Slovic, *The Construction of Preference*, 1st edn (Cambridge University Press, 2006), pp. 446–7. I wonder if further personalization/humanization could change the results even more. For example, what would be the result if psychiatrists were asked to release a patient with information that "20 out of 100 similar patients likely will commit an act of violence against a psychiatrist."
2. R. David Thomas, *Dave's Way*, rep. edn (Berkley, 1992).
3. Robert Cialdini is a professor of Psychology at Arizona State University and has spent many years devoted to research of persuasion techniques. Author of *Influence* (Collins, 2006).
4. The Rainbow vacuum company's website is rainbowsystem.com
5. John Stack's story was reported in *SmartMoney* (January 2004), p. 98.
6. Eric Anderson and Duncan Simester, "Mind Your Pricing Cues," *Harvard Business Review* (September 2003), pp. 96–103.
7. "Price-endings in China: When Numbers are Not Just Numbers," *China Entrepreneur*, monthly column (5 September 2005), p. 23.
8. Anderson and Simester, "Mind Your Pricing Cues."
9. Ibid.
10. Brian Grow and Keith Epstein, "The Poverty Business," *Business Week* (21 May 2007), pp. 57–66.
11. Tim Harford, The Undercover Economist: Exposing Why the Rich Are Rich, Why the Poor Are Poor– And Why You Can Never Buy a Decent Used Car! (Oxford University Press, 2006), pp. 31–4.

# 16   Distribution

## Key messages to whet your appetite

▶ Efficiency is not a natural outcome
▶ Individual rationality is bad for joint results
▶ Be the mafia of your distribution system

## Managing outside your company

*Successful marketing demands successful management of markets. We must manage the marketing function both inside our company and also outside our company, managing also those who are not our employees but nevertheless are busy distributing, selling, buying, consuming, and disposing of our products. Value increasingly is produced by groups of companies working together. The remaining chapters in this book all touch on this main point.*

*In this chapter on distribution I show why efficiency is not the natural outcome when companies work together. I use distribution as an example, but the example holds in all situations where independent decision-makers work together, be it a company and its distributors, its end-customers, its advertising agencies, its banks, and so on.*

*I argue that efficiency is not the most important thing in managing outside your company. Power is most important. If you manage your power well, this will help you to force greater efficiency throughout the network of companies of which you are a part, benefiting all members and your own company.*

## The key problem in distribution

The key problem in distribution is sub-optimization, meaning that members of any distribution system optimize their own performance, not the

151

performance of the system overall. When any member of a distribution channel spends marketing money, such spending increases profits for all members of the channel. Yet, any member makes marketing spending decisions based only on the increases in his own profit.

Suppose a manufacturer spends $100,000 on an advertising campaign and finds that the resulting additional sales generate additional profit of $80,000. The manufacturer discontinues the advertising campaign since spending $100,000 to get $80,000 is bad business. However, the additional sales generated by the advertising also increase profits for the distributors of the product, say by $80,000. If the manufacturer and distributors were one company, the advertising would be a success; spending $100,000 to get $160,000 is good business. But since they are not one company, the advertising will be discontinued.

One solution is for distributors and manufacturers to combine promotional monies. For example Cisco and its distributors contribute to a joint marketing fund. But such a negotiated solution requires careful negotiation, close cooperation, and trust. There are many companies in our value chain, all with different priorities, resources, time horizons, and so on. The problem with negotiated solutions, compared to free-market solutions, is that they need to be negotiated, and counterparts need to be willing to negotiate.

Distributors also make decisions on the amount of marketing money to put in. Customers that are too small or too far away to be profitable for the distributors are ignored. If profits for the manufacturer were taken into account also, then fewer customers would be ignored.

So the manufacturer stops advertising too soon and the distributor stops distributing too soon. Total profits are not optimized. If manufacturer and distributor were one company they would spend more on both advertising and distribution. But they are not one company.

Pricing too suffers from the sub-optimization problem. Suppose on a product selling for $100 the manufacturer earns $10 for each unit sold and the distributor earns $10 for each unit sold. Now suppose a customer comes to the distributor and offers to double his orders from the distributor, provided the distributor gives him an $8 discount on each item. Will the distributor give the discount? Of course not. Double sales can't compensate for the 80 percent reduction in profit on each unit sold. Total profit for the two players would increase if the distributor were to give the discount. But the distributor counts only the distributor profits.

Product design too suffers from the sub-optimization problem. Manufacturers design the kind of products that are easy and cheap to manufacture and easy to sell. They focus less on designing products that are easy to service and use. Pontiac's Montana minivan, for example, had to be lifted up in order to reach the spark plugs, which could only be changed from underneath. How could this happen? Because the benefits of easy to service and use go first and more directly to the distributor and to the end-customer.

The more players in your vertical marketing system, the more severe the sub-optimization problem. And these days the number of players involved in the production and distribution of any one product is on the increase due to today's and tomorrow's outsourcing trend. So it becomes increasingly important that we manage this problem. How do we do this? That will be our next topic.

> *When groups of companies cooperate, efficiency is not the natural outcome.*

## Distribution as a prisoner's dilemma

The sub-optimization problem faced by players in a distribution channel is not unlike that of the prisoner's dilemma. Suppose you and I commit a crime and we get caught. If we both don't confess, we both have to go to jail for five years. But the police, after putting us in separate cells, come to you with an offer. If you confess you get to go home tonight, while I have to go to jail for 20 years. They also come to my cell with the same offer. But they warn us that if we both confess, we both go to jail for ten years. Should I confess? Should you?

> If you do confess, I have to confess, too. It is better that I go to jail for ten years instead of 20 years.

> And if you do not confess, I should confess, also. This way I will go to jail for zero years instead of five years.

The decision is easy. No need to guess what you will do. Whatever you do, it is always better for me if I just confess. You make the same calculation, you also confess, and as a result we both go to jail for ten years (instead of five years if we had both shut our mouth). We both feel stupid, but we were both rational.

> *Individually rational decisions don't necessarily yield jointly rational results.*

The prisoner's dilemma is an interesting problem for game theorists in economics, but for criminals it is a real problem, increasing their cost of doing business. So how do criminals address the problem? Criminals join the Mafia. The Mafia says, "If you confess we will kill you." This threat changes my calculation and yours too. We both don't confess, and we both go to jail for five years instead of ten. Once we get out we say, "Thank you, Mr. Mafia, for threatening to kill us if we confessed." Thus, the Mafia adds value by reducing our cost. In return we donate part of our revenues to the Mafia.

Channel members are in much the same position as the prisoners in the prisoner's dilemma. Everyone is better off by looking out for number one; but if everyone looks out for number one, everyone suffers. The solution is simple: whether you are distributor or retailer or manufacturer, you try to be the Mafia of your channel system. All members of the system will be happier than if there is no Mafia, and you will be happiest of all.

> *Be the Mafia of your channel system.*

The more power you have over other members of the channel, to force channel members to do things they would not do of their own will, the more you can solve the problem of sub-optimization, to the benefit of all and especially yourself. Power receives rather little attention in business literature. It should receive a lot more attention. Preferably this should be intelligent attention. The attention power has received in marketing literature on the topic doesn't pass that test.

## Power in channels: marketing's view

Power in channels has received a lot of attention in the marketing literature. Marketing is particularly proud of its accomplishments in this area of intellectual endeavor. I remember being introduced, as a Ph.D. student, with some reverence to this "body of literature" as being particularly rich.

Unfortunately, the result of all that academic work says more about marketing's status as a relevant science than about channels. There is a suspicion among practitioners that academic theory is not always so relevant. In business, as opposed to, say, in physics, the word "theory" has come to mean the opposite of "reality." Marketing's literature on power in channels does a great job to justify business people's suspicions of academics as impractical fools.

Marketing literature borrowed its definition of power from sociology,[1] which had defined power, broadly speaking, as either the power to punish or the power to reward. This is a bit of a counterintuitive definition since it means, for example, that a slave has reward power over his master. Be that as it may, this was the definition of power adopted in sociology.

Consistent with its definition of power in this way, sociology also established the following axiom: the power of A over B is exactly equal to the power of B over A. The master and the slave by sociology's definition of power are exactly equal in power; the punishment power of the one is balanced by the reward power of the other. Of course, the definition does not reflect the common-sense notion of power, but defined this way it is consistent.

Then marketing borrows the definition of power from sociology, excitedly distinguishing punishment from reward power, but overlooks the implication of the definition, the essence of the definition, namely, that two parties are always equal in power.[2] Instead, marketing spends much effort over many years measuring who has more power in, for example, manufacturer–distributor relationships, and on which source of power gives you more power.

Much of this research was done in the 1970s and predictably and obediently finds the politically correct result of those times, namely, that reward power works better than punishment power. (The problem of all social science is that it must be socially acceptable. When ten out of ten academic studies prove that A is better than B, there are several competing explanations for such a result: (1) ten out of ten studies performed proved that A is better; (2) of 100 studies, 90 proved that B is better, but these studies were not publishable, (3) ten studies were done where the researchers falsified their data to prove A is better in order to get published. Today we laugh at 18th-century craniology and its study of skull shapes and character traits. Don't laugh too hard.)

An example of the odd thinking generated by this basic error in marketing's treatment of power is found on page 260 in a collection of advanced thinking in marketing titled *Kellogg on Marketing* (the Kellogg Business School belongs to Northwestern University and is world class in marketing):

For example, a manufacturer may identify [that] the distributorship is exerting too little sales effort on behalf of the manufacturer's product line ... Analysis might reveal that the effort level is low because the distributor makes more profit from selling a competitor's product, ... the manufacturer might use some of its *power to reward* [emphasis added] the distributor by increasing the distributor's discount [giving more of the profit to the distributor].[3]

It is common sense that when the distributor increases his margins at the expense of the manufacturer, this is not a case of the manufacturer successfully exercising "reward" power. Rather, it is a case of the distributor successfully using (punishment) power to squeeze more money from the manufacturer. Since we can't rely on marketing literature to tell us about power in channels, I'll do the heavy lifting myself.[4]

> *Giving money to your distributor does not show your power.*

### ✍ POINTS TO REMEMBER

☞ **When groups of companies cooperate, efficiency is not the natural outcome.**
☞ **Individually rational decisions don't necessarily yield jointly rational results.**
☞ **Be the Mafia of your channel system.**
☞ **Giving money to your distributor does not show your power.**

## Notes

1. John R.P. French and Bertram Raven, "Bases of Social Power," in Dorwin Cartwright, *Studies in Social Power* (University of Michigan Press, 1959); Richard M. Emerson, "Power Dependence Relations," *American Sociological Review*, Vol. 27 (February 1962), pp. 31–41.
2. I suspect that one marketing professor originally borrowed sociology's definition of power from the article "Bases of Social Power" by French and Raven without reading the whole article. Numerous professors in marketing have quoted one another and quoted the article but I wonder if anyone has ever read the article.
3. Dawn Iacobucci, *Kellogg on Marketing* (Wiley, 2000).
4. Marketing literature in general has failed dismally in its sycophantic attempts to impress marketing practitioners. Almost every academic article in marketing obediently creates a little section entitled "Managerial

Implications." Yet everybody in marketing knows that "practitioners neither subscribe to nor read academic marketing journals" (Shelby D. Hunt, "Marketing as a Profession: On Closing Stakeholder Gaps," *European Journal of Marketing*, 36(3) (2002), pp. 305–12). The only debate among marketing academics is on whether we should care. (For example, Alan Tapp, "Why Practitioners Don't Read Our Articles and What We Should Do About It," *The Marketing Review*, 5(1) (2005), pp. 3–13.) Meanwhile, in an amusing excess of creative writing, the American Marketing Association proudly asserts on its website: "Starting six decades ago and right up to today, marketers have been reading the *Journal of Marketing* for thought-provoking, in-depth articles."

# 17 Power

**Key messages to whet your appetite**

▶ Hard work doesn't pay
▶ Power pays
▶ Assume the tasks that increase your power

## Who gets the money?

*We always try to make our companies more efficient and more effective. However, efficiency and effectiveness are not the only thing, and not even the most important thing. Power is more important. Put simply: efficiency and effectiveness decide how much money there will be. Power decides who gets the money.*

*Of course, that is a little too simple. Power can also be a source of efficiency, for example, by solving the prisoner's dilemma in channels as we just saw. Conversely, efficiency can also be a source of power. If you have lower costs than your competitors, you can credibly threaten a price war. The power supplied to you by your efficiency dissuades potential competitors from coming too close to you.*

*Power can come from any number of other sources too, such as patents, a strong brand name, ownership of key assets, and so on. When we make our business decisions, it is important to look beyond efficiency considerations and pay as much, or more, attention to issues of power and control.*

*As mentioned earlier, power receives very little attention in business literature. I am not sure why. I think it might be that power as a construct has a negative aura. Power corrupts, and so on. But negative aura or not, it is better to have power than to not have power. That's why I include this chapter.*

## Who will be rich? Who will be poor?

In a free market economy, how do we divide the money? How do we decide who will be rich and who will be poor? When I ask students, some will suggest that how much money you get depends on "how hard you work." Other students are quick to scoff at such a notion, but actually the relationship between hard work and how much money you get is very strong. It just happens to be a strongly negative relationship.

The main rule for dividing income is that the less work you do, the more money you get. Thus, if you see someone working really hard, outside in the hot sun, pushing a wheelbarrow loaded with heavy bricks, you know that person is not earning very much money. Managers drinking coffee as they sit in their comfortable chairs in their air-conditioned offices, they make much more money. Tiger Woods never worked a day in his life. He retired and started playing golf when he was two years old. That's why he gets the most money of all.

> *There is a negative relationship between work and income.*

Some people might say that this does not seem very fair. But fair or unfair, the genius and justification of capitalism, and its Darwin-ordained survival, lies in its productivity, not in its fairness. Unfairness is very efficient. People who work hard all the time are too busy and tired anyway to spend money. Much more efficient, therefore, to give money to people who have the time to enjoy the money. My own household works that way too, very efficiently. Why is it true that the people who work the most receive the least money? The reason is that the underlying force is power. If I have power over you I want two things: first, I want you to do my work for me so I won't get so tired working. Second, I want you to give me your money so I can go spend it while you do my work. Power is the variable that drives the negative relationship of work and money.

> *Companies should give greater consideration to managing for power.*

## Managing for power

Going back to sociology and our discussion of the prisoner's dilemma, it is clear we want to maximize our punishment power rather than our reward power. According to sociology the power of the man holding the gun, saying, "Your money or your life," is balanced by the power of the other man to give his wallet or not. While the power may be equal, I prefer to hold the gun rather than the wallet.

Accordingly, any company must optimize the efficiency and effectiveness of the channel system – maximize the pie – but also manage the balance of power inside the channel system to the company's advantage, maximizing the company's share of the pie. After all, what good is efficiency if you cannot capture the rewards?

> *Slaves do not benefit from efficiency.*

Any company needs a certain amount of profit to keep doing what it does, but any company also tries to achieve profits above and beyond that minimum acceptable amount of profit. The balance of power among companies working together decides who best exceeds that minimum acceptable amount.

Looking back at the example above from *Kellogg on Marketing*, a distributor might decide to represent additional manufacturers even without expectation of additional profit from those manufacturers, simply to shift the balance of power vis-à-vis currently represented manufacturers in its favor. The payoff for the distributor comes when he then forces the currently represented manufacturers to give him a greater share of the channel system's profits. Marketing's academic channel literature considers the manufacturer's victimization, his yielding of profits, a triumph of the manufacturer's reward power; I consider it a manufacturer's failure to manage power.

Generally speaking, the secret to creating the right kind of power – the secret to holding the gun rather than the wallet – is to create dependency on the part of other players. Once you have created dependency you can extract your rewards. Note that rewards to other players can serve as an excellent tool to create dependency on their part. But these must be rewards of a special nature, the kind that create dependency.

A department store chain in Hong Kong, for example, offered a manufacturer expanded display space and promised a significant sales increase provided the manufacturer stop selling through competing stores. The manufacturer wisely declined this generous offer, worrying that a year later the store might insist on a significant increase in its margins.

> *Manage relationships to maximize your partners' dependence on you.*

A big question in distribution is always: how much of the distribution task should a company do and which parts can be done by channel members? In answering this question, a company should not merely look at efficiency. Based on our earlier discussion, we can see that a company should take on those distribution tasks that preserve and build its power over the channel. In this way, the company both can force behaviors by other channel members that will improve efficiency of the channel and it can capture more than its fair share of the rewards from that efficiency.

> *Perform those functions in the channel that increase your power.*

Distributors generally try to keep manufacturers in the dark about how and where they sell the manufacturer's products. Obviously this is a wise policy on their part. Information is power and power is money. Conversely, smart manufacturers should invest to become expert on the channel despite the channel's reluctance to share information, and they should be willing to invest in information collection to increase their power over the channel.

Promotion too can help increase your power to avoid getting squeezed by your channel partners. For example, suppose you are a manufacturer of a grocery store product and supermarkets are increasing their power against you by merging with one another. Suppose, further, that your brand is not powerful enough to get customers to take notice if the supermarket drops you. What do you do? You could implement a repeat purchase promotion where repeat purchasers of your product can save a piece of the product packaging and over time save up enough pieces to get gifts for free. Suppose that the promotion costs you money, has zero effect on sales, and only 10 percent of your customers take part. Is the promotion a failure?

From the perspective of promotion as a promotion tool, yes. However, from the perspective of promotion as a distribution tool to increase power vis-à-vis the supermarket, the promotion may be a success. If the supermarket stops selling your brand, it risks losing some proportion of your customers who are loyal to your sales promotion. If only 2 percent of your customers will go to another store so they can complete their saving of your pieces of packaging to qualify for their free gift, then the supermarket cannot afford to kick you out. A purchasing manager for a supermarket chain prefers not to be held responsible by the store manager for lost customers (or complaining customers) just because he got deadlocked in his attempts to beat you down on price. The lesson for stores is that they should be careful about the kinds of promotions they let manufacturers run.

It has been shown that in-store sales promotions typically lose money for the manufacturer.[1] The sales increases do not justify the expense. Manufacturers, of course, are well aware of this. Yet manufacturers persist in spending increasing amounts of money on sales promotions. Perhaps the justification is not the promotion effect, but the effect on the balance of power between manufacturers and increasingly powerful retailers.

*Any P can improve any C: promotion can increase channel power.*

## ✍ POINTS TO REMEMBER

- ☞ **There is a negative relationship between work and income.**
- ☞ **Companies should give greater consideration to managing for power.**
- ☞ **Slaves do not benefit from efficiency.**
- ☞ **Manage relationships to maximize your partners' dependence on you.**
- ☞ **Perform those functions in the channel that increase your power.**
- ☞ **Any P can improve any C: promotion can increase channel power.**

## Note

1. John Philips Jones, "The Double Jeopardy of Sales Promotions," *Harvard Business Review* (September/October 1990).

# 18 A New Idea in Marketing: Honesty

---

## Key messages to whet your appetite

▶ Honesty is a most valuable asset
▶ Dishonesty is a very slippery slope
▶ Stealing money is wrong, so is stealing time
▶ Would you do this to your mother?

---

## Marketing and honesty

*Marketing and honesty are like toothache and fun. In the popular perception, people in marketing may not be as bad as lawyers or criminals, but we are no engineers either.*

*The suspicion of marketing is old. In ancient Greece, where different professions had their own gods, merchants and thieves shared Hermes, a god with little wings at his feet to help him get away faster. The merchant who buys an egg for 2 cents and sells it for 4 cents has always been seen as a thief, unlike the farmer who in fact steals the egg from a chicken. The suspicion is not about to go away: "Would You Want Your Daughter to Marry a Marketing Man?" is the title of a long-ago article in the Journal of Marketing (written when the possibility that "your daughter" might be a marketing woman was still a way off).[1] More recently,* All Marketers Are Liars *has been a bestseller.[2]*

*Maybe all marketers are liars but that does not mean that you should be one too. In this chapter I introduce the idea that honesty and a reputation for honesty might be a valuable asset. I start with the amazing story of the Longaberger Company.*

# The Longaberger Company

The Longaberger Company must rank among one of the most improbable business success stories ever.[3] The company makes baskets woven out of thin wood strips. These baskets were very popular in the 19th century, around 1880 or so. You can use such a basket to carry your food if you go on a picnic or you can put one on a table and look at it.

We are talking about a company in an industry that was mostly obsolete once plastic was invented. The Longaberger Company was started in the 1970s by a man, Dave Longaberger, who took nine years to complete six years of high school, mostly because he never became very good at reading. Over a 25-year period he built his company into a $700 million in sales and 8,000 employees phenomenon. He became quite famous when he decided to build his new six-story headquarters in the shape of a wooden basket.

So what was Mr. Longaberger's secret? Put simply, he was ruthlessly honest. Dave Longaberger was the type of old-fashioned man who believes that truth is important and that lying to customers is no joking matter, even if it improves sales and profits.

In our lives there are moments where we take one road or another, and then we can't go back any more. Sometimes we take the right road, sometimes we don't. The same is true for companies. Let us see where Longaberger and his company took the right road.

Dave Longaberger learned basket making from his father, who made baskets for his mother to use for grocery shopping, for laundry, to hold bread at the dinner table, to hold fruit, and so on. Dave sold his baskets through stores at first. But then one buyer of his baskets, Charleen Cuckovich, convinced him that she could sell the baskets with a sales system similar to the way Amway and Shaklee do business. She proved extremely successful in selling the baskets and in recruiting additional people to sell even more baskets.

One day Dave Longaberger attended Charleen's sales presentation. During the presentation she told a story about each of the baskets. One basket, she explained, was used by the Longaberger children to gather eggs from their henhouse, and was designed to hold exactly twelve eggs. The audience was very charmed by this story, especially when it was demonstrated that indeed the basket could hold exactly 12 eggs. The sales meeting was very successful. But Dave Longaberger didn't look too happy afterwards. Finally, Charleen said: "Well, what do you think?" He answered: "We never had any chickens!" They both laughed. But then he told her seriously: "Stick to the facts next time."[4]

Was this a small moment in the history of the company? I don't think so. Here was a fork in the road. The true story of the company is that its products are made by hand by real people, following the traditional ways of basket-making that Dave Longaberger learned from watching his father. Sure, we can laugh about a chicken story when there never were any chickens, but when we add a few untrue stories to the true stories, when only 90 percent of the stories we tell are true, then every story we tell may or may not be true. Dave Longaberger set in stone an important principle: honesty and truth are more important than a good sales story.

The company's sales and success are built entirely on the enthusiasm and dedication of independent salespeople who organize parties to sell the baskets. I have no doubt that the reputation and reality of truth and honesty were tremendously valuable in recruiting dedicated sales people for the company and in making sales people more effective. As Mormons will tell you, anyone can be a great salesperson when they truly believe in what they sell.

But better salespeople and more sales is not the only benefit of company honesty. Here is another benefit: if employees of a company know that the company will not lie to customers to achieve greater profits, employees know that the company more than likely also will not lie to employees to achieve greater profits.

I said earlier that, for example, Carl Sewell built his company on the idea that any P can improve any C. It is also true that any business function can improve any other business function. For example, things we do in marketing can improve the success of the HR department. Honesty in your marketing likely improves the quality of the people you can hire and their dedication to their work and your company.

At one point the Longaberger Company was in serious financial trouble. To save the company Dave Longaberger asked the independent salespeople and distributors to accept lower commissions. Everyone accepted the lower commissions not just without protest but with messages of support. Why? Because they knew Dave Longaberger was telling the truth when he said that the company would go under unless they would help him. Honesty and a reputation for honesty are assets that we don't put on the balance sheet, but they are very real nonetheless. Sometimes they save your company.

> *Honesty is a most valuable corporate asset.*

The recent bestseller on marketing entitled *All Marketers Are Liars*[5] explains that often marketing's job is the telling of stories that help people lie to themselves, to convince themselves that they need products that in fact they don't need. Some students in a similar vein have argued to me that honesty and truth are outdated, that truth lies in the eye of the beholder anyway, that you have to lie today to survive because everybody lies. I think the opposite is true. Last time I checked, scarcity increases rather than decreases a commodity's value.

When all marketers are acknowledged liars you should be the last one standing who is still telling the truth. So how honest is your company?

> *How honest do your customers, your investors, your employees think your company is?*

## You can't compartmentalize honesty or dishonesty

Honesty is not compartmentalizable. Longaberger cut short even the smallest whiff of dishonesty to customers. Thereby he brought a level of trust and honesty to all relationships of the company. When you are dishonest to your employees, that dishonesty will not be contained either. The dishonesty will affect all relationships the company has internally and externally.

Bob Nardelli's tenure at Home Depot serves as a warning: He gained fame as CEO of Home Depot after he lost out in the race to succeed Jack Welch. As CEO of Home Depot he managed to increase the stock price by about 6 percent over six years (half of that increase on his last day when it was announced that he was fired). During that same time, direct competitor Lowe's went up 250 percent. What went wrong at Home Depot?

Nardelli, who received pay of as much as $100 million in a single year, justified his reward for no performance by saying that if you looked at sales and costs and profits numbers, and so on, he had achieved a great deal; he couldn't be responsible for the stock price. Let us listen to a Home Depot customer, Scott Burns, who happens to write articles for MSN money central:[6]

Is Home Depot Shafting Shoppers? ... Home Depot is a consistent abuser of its customer's time ... my wife and I loved Home Depot, the stores were staffed with well-trained, knowledgeable and helpful people. Today it's difficult to find a staff person at a Home Depot ... I've left the store empty-handed after a hopeless wait. My wife has gotten so frustrated waiting – while trying to buy carpeting for an entire house – that she's taken her business elsewhere. [Home Depot] abuses our time.

Note that the customer feels shafted. He feels robbed of a store he loved. He feels his time is abused. Nardelli's numbers are not real. Home Depot cashed in its brand equity. Experienced full-time workers were replaced with cheaper part-time workers, bonuses for customer service were sharply reduced, customer service was minimized. By 2006 Home Depot had achieved the dead last position in the University of Michigan customer satisfaction survey of major retailers.[7] Sales in the last quarter of 2006 fell by more than 20 percent.

It's a problem of false accounting. It's not the sort of false accounting of hiding debts, faking income, selling off assets secretly, and paying accountants to cover up the evil deeds. Bob Nardelli engaged in a more subtle form of cooking the books. Brand equity and customer loyalty, important assets though they may be, do not appear on a company's balance sheet. If you cash in assets that are not on the balance sheet you magically produce money out of thin air.

Nardelli may have fooled himself into believing he was accomplishing great things, but he didn't fool the stock market. The stock price went nowhere despite Nardelli's busy production of better numbers. Nardelli didn't just fool himself though. As the curtain was closing on Nardelli in 2006, very admiring articles appeared in *Harvard Business Review, Business Week*, and *Fast Company*.[8] (Obviously the authors weren't Home Depot shoppers, or employees, or shareholders.)

Veteran Home Depot employees were robbed of jobs they thought were safe. The employees added significant value. Their jobs should have been safe. But firing them could increase profits before it would decrease profits. Customers, as a result, were cheated out of a store they loved, out of hours of wasted time, and out of needed advice on what materials and tools to use. Shareholders ended up robbed of what should have been great share performance during a housing boom. You can't compartmentalize honesty or dishonesty. When you rob your employees, you rob customers too, and finally shareholders too.

When I speak about dishonesty here, I don't mean that Nardelli is not an honest man. Nothing about him, or written about him, casts any doubt about his personal integrity. That is why you must ask other people: how honest is my company? Don't think: "Well, I'm honest, so anyone who questions what my company does is wrong."

*Dishonesty is a very slippery slope.*

I recommended earlier that you should make yourself suffer the way you make your customers suffer. *Fast Company* describes how Nardelli could watch on camera the stores and people in the stores in real time from his office. Now here is what he should have done. He should have watched just one customer waiting in line for 30 minutes. Throughout the 30 minutes Nardelli should have stood still and done nothing, just waited. He should have done this twice a day. Maybe this way he could have avoided the customer service disaster for which Home Depot is now famous.

*Remember to suffer like you make your customers suffer.*

## Shafting our customers

I think the way Scott Burns phrased his complaint about Home Depot very interesting. He was "shafted." Many companies slide into a habit of robbing their customers. It happens because the logic or tyranny of the financial markets demands ever-rising profits and sales. Sooner or later such demands run into a physical, or market, or other limit. As a result, companies go through a cycle of exceeding, meeting, and finally cheating customer expectations.

Short-staffing is one way to rob customers. Companies are robbing our time when they save money by putting us in long lines at the checkout counter, and in even much longer lines at the customer service counter, or keep us waiting at the phone for half an hour or more, especially when interrupting such a long wait repeatedly with commercial messages. It's kidnapping. It's time robbery.

*Stealing money is wrong, so is stealing time.*

I mentioned at the outset of this book that in too many companies managers can get a promotion when they figure out a way to cut costs by $1 for the company at the expense of an extra $100 in costs for customers.

When companies are upfront about what they charge customers, this may be merely unwise. When companies hide the extra time and money they charge customers, they slide into "shafting" customers, robbing customers. In either case, industries become vulnerable to newcomers who decide to increase their own cost by $1 and save customers $100. Remember how the personal computer industry dug its own grave, and built Dell's mountain, by taking weeks to fix customers' computers.

> *Stealing money and time from your customers is risky business.*

## Would you do this to your mother?

Witness also the airline industry. Discount airlines such as Southwest, People Express, Valujet, Jetblue, and so on find it easy to establish their brands and make them popular with customers. Why is it so easy?

Because the big advertising campaigns by established players don't create customer loyalty. Frequent-flyer programs also don't create loyalty. Good service creates loyalty. I mentioned earlier that airlines don't care what happens to you after you get off the plane. But do they care while you're on the plane?

I'm not just talking about the silly swimming vests (do boats carry parachutes?). Northwestern kept passengers for seven hours and longer on its planes during a snowstorm. Snowstorms happen and using the slides to evacuate the plane costs money. I understand that. But Northwest kept charging its starving prisoners monopoly prices for drinks and food until passengers revolted outright and helped themselves.[9] Here is something I don't understand. Why spend millions on advertising and then try to earn a few extra hundred dollars at the expense of an avalanche of bad publicity? Northwestern isn't alone. Increased incidents of air rage are blamed on society's deterioration in public civility. Maybe part of the problem lies in airlines' deterioration in public civility?

> *Here is a simple standard of customer service: would you do this to your mother?*

Where there is air rage, soon there will be bank rage. The banking industry now has reached the stage where customer robbery has become necessary to achieve above-average sales and profit increase every year.

The industry has become addicted to what Fred Reichheld calls "bad profits," the kind of sneaky revenue enhancers that make customers hate you.[10]

My son, who is a student, checked his near-zero bank balance before using his card to buy gas. But there was a $1.50 charge for checking his balance. As a result he went 50 cents negative. This resulted in a $39 overdraft charge. Maintaining a negative balance cost him a further $7 per day. Imagine his unhappy surprise when he opened his bank statement some ten days later to find a negative balance of more than $100. While the bank saw no profit in informing him of his negative balance, they had meanwhile sent an e-mail offering a credit card. He decided to stick to credit unions and Internet stockbrokers for the rest of his life. He also decided to ask for more money from his stingy father.

My son's story is just one small story. It is easy to find much bigger and much worse stories. Take, for example, private student loans, often co-marketed by banks and universities, with the banks hiding in the sheep's clothing of the university's financial aid office. Students graduate and find they have to come up with 18 percent interest payments. Bankruptcy is not allowed on these loans thanks to astute lobbying by the industry.

The financial industry is on a treadmill of finding ever more ingenious ways to trap and trick customers. But it's a suicidal treadmill. A new bank will have little trouble luring customers away from the industry today. Note the huge success of ING Direct USA, for example, with its selling point: "no bank fees, no minimum balances, no hidden catches."[11] It is also easy to see that sooner or later public pressure will exceed lobbyists' campaign contributions and new rules to protect consumers will be passed.

Holland's ABN AMRO comes to mind as an early warning. The bank invented creative new obscure fees, closed branches, and laid off employees, informing customers that "to increase the quality and efficiency of our service to you we have closed the branch near your home."

Five years into a much-heralded effort to double the stock price by robbing customers and reducing services, after the stock price never moved, despite higher profits, a hedge fund demanded that the bank be split up and sold off, the hapless CEO is in trouble with shareholders, and both the best employees and the best customers are on the run. When you rob your customers, only desperate or dumb customers will be your long-term viable customers. Good luck building a great business on that. Good luck too on finding great employees to help you do it. How honest is your company? How honest is your pricing? How honest is your advertising? How honest is your sales story?

You are not convinced yet? Think of Blockbuster. Why didn't they immediately copy Netflix when they saw how well that model for renting movies worked? They had many advantages over Netflix: capital, inventory, customers and their addresses, connections with the studios, the brand name, the means of communication through their stores, and so on. I will tell you why.

Under the Netflix model of renting movies you never pay a late fee. Blockbuster was addicted to its juicy late fees, a source of extra profit, which had been much enhanced by confusing customers through offering one-, two-, and five-day rentals. Copying Netflix would mean no more late fees. Meanwhile, those much-beloved late fees proved its Achilles heel when Netflix started out promoting its business model with its promise of "No late fees, ever."

Blockbuster knew of the anger its late-fee policies created. Its commercial announcing the end of Blockbuster's late fees ridiculously showed an angry crowd in front of a Blockbuster store chanting "No more late fees." (Like any real addict, Blockbuster could not give up late fees after all. Blockbuster franchisees quickly came up with new late fees under a different name).

Perhaps you think that I'm just doing a little ivory tower talking here about honesty? I'm not. Sure, marketing's job is to seduce the customer and I have shown lots of ways of seduction. But there is a line between seducers on the one hand and conmen on the other hand. If you are not sure where the line lies, here is a simple way to find out. Ask your customers whether they tell or would tell a friend to do business with you. Ask your customers if they think you are an honest company. (If you're a bank charging $39 overdraft fees, or an airline charging a $100 lost ticket fee, or you keep customers waiting on the phone for more than 15 minutes when your product fails, don't waste time asking. Your customers hate you. Google "I hate your name".)

When you decide on your policies, ask yourself: would I do this to my mother? Pursue honesty, the latest and greatest innovation in marketing. You were looking for new ways of differentiation? Now you know a new way.

*Honesty: a whole new idea.*

✍ **POINTS TO REMEMBER**

☞ **Honesty is a most valuable corporate asset.**
☞ **How honest do your customers, your investors, your employees think your company is?**
☞ **Dishonesty is a very slippery slope.**
☞ **Remember to suffer like you make your customers suffer.**
☞ **Stealing money is wrong, so is stealing time.**
☞ **Stealing money and time from your customers is risky business.**
☞ **Would you do this to your mother?**
☞ **Honesty: a whole new idea.**

## Notes

1. Richard N. Farmer, "Would You Want Your Daughter to Marry a Marketing Man?" *Journal of Marketing*, 31(1) (January 1967), pp. 1–3.
2. Seth Godin, *All Marketers Are Liars* (Portfolio Hardcover, 2005).
3. David H. Longaberger and Robert L. Shook, *Longaberger: An American Success Story* (Collins, 2003).
4. Ibid.
5. Godin, *All Marketers Are Liars*.
6. Scott Burns, "Is Home Depot Shafting Shoppers?" articles.moneycentral.msn (8 March 2007).
7. "Satisfaction Not Guaranteed," *Business Week* (19 June 2006).
8. Ram Charan, "Home Depot's Blueprint for Culture Change", *Harvard Business Review* (1 April 2006); Jennifer Reingold, "Bob Nardelli is Watching," *Fast Company* (December 2005), p. 76; "Renovating Home Depot," *Business Week* (6 March 2006), p. 50.
9. Susan Carey, "Snow-stranded Passengers Rap Northwest Over Chaos in Detroit," *The Wall Street Journal* (8 January 1999), B1.
10. Fred Reichheld, The Ultimate Question: Driving Good Profits and True Growth (Harvard Business School Press, 2006).
11. Arbara Kiviat, "How a Man On a Mission (And a Harley) Reinvented Banking," *Time*, 169(26) (25 June 2007), p. 44.

# 19 Outside Your Company

## Key messages to whet your appetite

▶ Add value throughout the value chain
▶ Do things that cost no money
▶ Don't be so busy
▶ Success in marketing is achieved outside the company

## Outside

*This final chapter argues that what we do outside our company is a lot more important than what we do on the inside. Unfortunately, we all feel more comfortable on the inside. I also point to the strange fact that companies seem to be least interested in those ideas that cost little or nothing to implement, or that actually save money, but that have significant positive impact on sales, profits, and customer satisfaction. I offer my own theory on why this might be so and suggest a remedy. Finally, I point to the fact that companies sometimes seem to be without management. There are people running around busily, giving speeches, holding meetings, but nothing happens, certainly nothing new happens. I point out that in the end we have to do things, we have to try things, we have to initiate action, we have to let the market decide, we have to give the market something to decide. Success is determined outside our company.*

## Manage outside your company too

A company's organization chart shows a pyramid of employees, setting the boundaries of the organization according to the legal nature of the employment relationship. Ask yourself: why are your salespeople on your organization chart but not your distributor's salespeople? Why is your VP for HR on your chart, but not the purchasing manager of the chain store who buys 40 percent of your output?

Use part of your R&D budget to find out exactly what happens with your product after it leaves your company. Build a chart identifying all relevant players involved in moving your product. That should be your organization chart.

> *Build and maintain an organization chart showing all players involved in moving your product.*

Once you have a chart that identifies all the relevant players inside and outside your company, set out to manage them. Make sure all people involved in the success of your product receive all pertinent information about your product, make sure all receive the support that can better enable and motivate them to make your product successful.

For example, a car company should send the salespeople of its dealerships a toy model of any new car and the calendar showing the car on that winding road with the leaves swirling, and so on. But a car company also should send the toy model and the calendar to the service people, mechanics, receptionists and secretaries of the dealerships. They too influence the image, quality experience, and sales of your cars.

I assume you don't forget your own secretary on Secretary's Day. Don't forget your distributor's secretary either. Think of this as simply being nice. Being nice costs you little, is good for your health, makes you feel good about yourself, improves the world you live in, and it pays well.

> *Everyone who influences the success of your product, directly or indirectly, should be treated as a valued customer.*

## Support your system

To treat our distributors' employees kindly is a minimum proposition. We could go much further and learn from Sage Software. Sage discovered that many of its software resellers had only one salesperson: the owner. Business owners proved tremendously reluctant to hire salespeople because they feared the costly risk of a salesperson not working out. They feared correctly: only 32 percent of salespeople lasted for more than one year; only 15 percent for more than two years. Resellers' reluctance to hire salespeople naturally cost Sage significant sales. Sage decided to do something about it. First, Sage offered $10,000 to resellers willing to hire a new salesperson, reducing the cost of hiring wrong. Second, Sage actively involved itself in the hiring process, creating a profile of top salespeople of Sage software around the country, providing tests to identify likely successful candidates, co-interviewing candidates, reducing the probability of hiring wrong.

A bit of science helped a lot: 78 percent of salespeople hired by Sage's resellers now last for more than one year; 65 percent last for more than two years. Sage did for its resellers what its resellers individually could not afford to do for themselves. It is all too easy to save a dollar ourselves by imposing a much greater cost on our customers. Sage went the other way, spending money and developing special expertise in order to significantly reduce its resellers' costs.[1]

> *When you help your channel, you help yourself.*

You might help a customer manage promotion too. I was at CompUSA once to buy a laptop. Various laptops were on display, but I saw no information on battery life. I asked a salesperson. He suggested that this information might be on the box and that the service department would have those boxes. Does CompUSA have a service department to remind customers not to expect service from the sales staff? I bought a Dell.

I should have done my research before going to the store. I was not a smart shopper. But the sale was still lost. A helpful salesperson could have found the information I wanted in the manual, on the box, or even on the Internet. But that didn't happen. If it had happened I could have filled out a special recognition card and the salesperson would have been the salesperson of the month. But if it takes an award-winning salesperson to make a sale, we have a problem.

Regular contact with salespeople in stores would alert a manufacturer to the problem. The salesperson I talked to, for example, knows that the lack of information about battery life is a problem. But it is not his job to educate the store or the manufacturer.

Marketing managers should spend time asking customers about any questions they might have in the course of selling and purchasing our products and then set out to answer those questions. A manufacturer could attach a sticker to its computers with clear answers to the battery question and other frequently asked questions. We can improve our service to the store, and improve the service inside the store, and provide education to salespeople and end-customers for 2 cents per computer.

Perhaps attaching more information to the laptop on display in the store will add only 1 percent to sales? I'll take any 1 percent I can get that I don't have to work hard for. Across industries, if companies increase sales by 1 percent, profits increase by 3 percent.[2]

> *Do the little things right; big things take care of themselves.*

Computer manufacturers today offer more in-store information but they are the exception. Stores are still filled with an overabundance of competing products of increasing complexity standing deaf and dumb next to one another, facing bewildered customers who are looking in vain for help from equally bewildered salespeople, provided there still are salespeople.

Ikea, the world's biggest furniture retailer, has both fewer employees on the floor and higher scores for customer satisfaction than the industry norm. How do they do it? Wim Neitzert, previously manager for Ikea, now a consultant to furniture retailers, tells how his clients believe that a good furniture store must have good salespeople. In response to Neitzert's question as to why good salespeople are necessary, retailers tell him salespeople are necessary to answer customers' questions.

Customers ask about prices, sizes, and colors. Ikea makes sure to have that information and any other relevant information on the product. It is both cheaper and it is superior service to have the information available on the product. Such a small thing, such huge savings, such happy customers, so much higher sales.[3]

Why do we so rarely look for little ways to help solve our big problems? Why have both manufacturers and stores not figured out that they could sell more by adding information? What are the marketing managers for the furniture manufacturers and for the furniture stores doing all day? Ikea makes a deliberate attempt to attach all information customers might need, but most other furniture stores do not.

Manufacturers are not managing the stores, they are not supporting the stores, they are not inside the stores, they don't see what is happening inside the stores. Meanwhile, though stores are following Ikea's example and reducing the number of salespeople, think Home Depot; they are not following Ikea's example in providing information in other ways. Nobody is minding the store, so to speak. This is a good opportunity for manufacturers, but it is not one they have jumped on.

I use a retail example here, but all companies have "stores." For pharmaceutical companies, for example, pharmacies, doctor's offices, and hospitals are the store. For a manufacturer of industrial machinery, exhibitions are the store. For a homebuilder, the realtors are his stores. For insurance companies the Internet and the phone and independent agents are the stores. Manage and control your stores.

Learn from Progressive's success story. Here was a company that truly understood that its selling job is to help people buy and that when you save customers time and money you will save money too. Its website and salespeople were the first to offer not only information on the Progressive prices, but a comparison with all other prices of competitors; a very radical and very successful initiative.[4]

> *Manage your stores.*

## It is better to give than to receive

Marketing managers might argue that the education of customers in the store is the job of the store, not the job of the manufacturer. Don't worry about who should do what. The only thing that matters is the success of our system and our ability to enjoy more of its fruits. Surprisingly, by trying to give to the system rather than receive, by focusing on the outside, on the success of other companies, not on our own success, we may help ourselves best. Let me show three examples of very successful companies who became successful by specifically focusing on the success of other companies.

In 1954, Ray Kroc started McDonald's. A large number of better-financed and more experienced competitors were already building the fast-food franchise industry. Ray Kroc followed (and then led) the industry in introducing factory-type scientific management methods to the restaurant industry.

But in one critical aspect Ray Kroc did not follow industry practice. As a salesman to the industry he knew how franchising companies saw franchisees as serfs who should be exploited at every opportunity. Ray Kroc saw a simpler truth. He wrote: "My belief was that I had to help the individual operator succeed in every way I could. His success would insure my success."[5] Ray Kroc therefore put in place McDonald's policy of never being a supplier to its franchisees, foregoing the traditionally major source of profit in the industry. According to Ray Kroc: "Once you get into the supply business you become more concerned about what *you* are making on sales to your franchisee than on how *his* sales are doing."

*If you steal from your friends, how many friends will you have?*

A very different company in a very different industry in a very different age had the same idea. Brightstar is a distributor and customizer of mobile phones started up by a young Bolivian immigrant by the name of Marcelo Claure.[6] Today Brightstar is "the world's largest wireless distribution and supply chain solutions company".[7] Sales went from $14 million in 1997, to $1,200 million in 2003, to more than $3,500 million in 2006.

What did Brightstar do right? It came up with a radical new business model summarized in two slogans. "We add value at all points of the wireless value chain." and "Our business model is to support your business model."

Ericsson made Brightstar its main distributor in South America in 1998. Ericsson's status in South America was reflected in its choice of minor player Brightstar as its main distributor. Ericsson was a very small player in South America with around 2 percent market share and its phones reportedly were unattractive and too expensive.

Brightstar decided to make Ericsson competitive by making it the easiest brand to do business with in Latin America: Brightstar delivered phones to the customer's doorstep all over Latin America. Brightstar customers were allowed more than 30 days to pay, had no minimum order requirement, and if they couldn't sell the phones they could always sell them back to Brightstar at a discount. Brightstar/Ericsson would move any overstocked or outdated phones from say Uruguay to Peru. Competing international brands left it to their South American customers to deal with the headaches of bringing products into South America.

Within 12 months of Brightstar becoming Ericsson's main distributor, sales for Ericsson doubled in South America. In 2000 Ericsson's contract with Brightstar expired. Motorola jumped at the opportunity to make Brightstar its distributor. Motorola's market share in South America went from 16 percent in 2000 to 33 percent in 2003.

Brightstar doesn't have workers and managers who are smarter and work harder than anybody else in the industry. Instead, this company has a different vision: *How can we add value throughout the value chain? How can we support our customers' business model?* Brightstar found good answers to that question both before its products reached its customers and, uniquely, even after its products reached its customers.

*Add value throughout the value chain. Worry first about your customers' business model.*

Whole industries could benefit from Brightstar's excellent question. *How can we add value throughout the value chain?* For example, medical errors are a huge problem in hospitals. One study showed that only 61.9 percent of heart attack patients receive a prescription for beta-blockers following a heart attack.[8] This is a medical error you might expect a beta-blocker manufacturer to get a heart attack about. How much have pharmaceutical companies spent on efforts to reduce error rates in hospitals?

The current major effort by the Institute for Healthcare Improvement (IHI) to reduce hospital error rates is led by charitable foundations, nurses associations, medical associations, government agencies, and health insurance companies.[9] By and large, pharmaceutical companies have not been involved in this effort. Implementation by some 3,000 hospitals of an error-reduction program developed by IHI saved about 122,000 lives over 18 months.[10] Those survivors can live to take another $5,000 or $10,000 or $20,000 worth of pharmaceutical products. Reduced errors in just one year could enhance pharmaceutical industry revenues by a billion or two in subsequent years. The pharmaceutical industry might want to allocate some of its R&D money to finding ways to eliminate hospital errors.

> *Solving your customers' problems solves your problems.*

Greg Wittstock also built his business, Aquascape Inc., on the principle that it is better to give than to receive.[11] Wittstock sells supplies to contractors who build ponds or small lakes for homeowners. Wittstock started by building ponds himself. He soon became very busy. This led him to standardize the process of building ponds. Next, he decides he should franchise his very successful business model. That did not work at all. Nobody bought a franchise.

So he decides he will give away what he had planned to sell: his building process knowledge, his marketing and pricing systems, and his product designs. He decides he will earn his money by selling supplies to the contractors who come to learn from him.

Could contractors come to his seminars to learn from him for free and then buy supplies elsewhere? Yes, contractors could, and perhaps in theory they should, but in reality most don't. They have good reason to stay loyal to him. Wittstock has a no-back-order-policy, meaning that his warehouse is always deliberately overstocked. If ever there is a customer who calls for a part and that part is not in inventory ready to be shipped, the flag flying in front of the building is lowered to half-staff. According to Wittstock: "If a $2 plumbing fitting is missing, the contractor can't hook up a pump ... a one day job turns into a two day job ... [and] you cut the contractor's profitability in half."

There are sophisticated formulas to calculate what a company's optimal inventory rate should be to maximize a *company's* profit, considering the cost of ordering, the cost of holding inventory, the opportunity cost of lost sales when an item is not in stock, and so on. But these formulas worry about the wrong thing. Wittstock gets it right. Wittstock worries about his *customers'* profits. He does not calculate what a stock-out costs *him*, he calculates what a stock-out costs *his customer*. His 35,000 customers are so loyal to Wittstock that competitors refer to his business as a cult.

*Sophisticated formulas don't help when you put in the wrong numbers.*

Ray Kroc sold franchises and refused to make money as a supplier to his franchisees. Claure focuses on what happens to his products after they have left his business. Wittstock gives away the franchise, but makes money as a supplier. Three different businesses, but they are identical in why people are so happy to give them money. People are so happy because Wittstock, Kroc, and Claure run their businesses in ways designed not to optimize their own profits; instead they run their business to optimize the profits of the members of their network: they look for opportunities to spend $10 if it will save network members $100. Unsurprisingly, people and companies push one another out of the way in order to join such a network.

*Maximizing your customers' profits maximizes your profits.*

Kroc, Claure, and Wittstock are not the norm. Companies prefer to push annoying problems outside the company on to customers and suppliers, and so on.

In an extreme example of saving a few dollars at a huge cost to customers, the State of Louisiana's Office of Motor Vehicles (OMV) discovered that on a total take of $800 million in fines and fees it lost some $120,000 net per year due to bad checks.

The OMV decided that everyone should pay with a certified check. Thus the state required several million people to buy certified checks at a cost of 50 –75 cents each (as well as spend time and gas to drive to the bank, stand in line, and so on) in order to save the state $120,000. In response to a storm of complaints politicians quickly forced an end to the policy. But when Home Depot does a similar thing, or your own company, where do people complain?

*Don't be the Louisiana Office of Motor Vehicles.*

## Something about small things

Many of the marketing actions and ideas that I talk about in this book cost little or no money, or even save money. Asking a customer for a glass of iced water doesn't cost much. Attaching information to a Persian rug about the thread count, the design, and so on, saves the store the cost of a salesperson. Attaching information about battery life saves the store a sale. Testing alternative advertising ideas costs little compared to the cost of lost sales and a lost company when a campaign has no effect. Offering three different set menus for lunch rather than two is a cheap way to increase the average sales amount. Eliminating check-in and check-out procedures for frequent guests would save hotels money.

I always wondered why companies don't do those little things that can greatly enhance revenues, profits, customer satisfaction, repeat business, and so on, but that cost little or no money, or even save money. Often, as in the case of Ikea, these are little things that are already proven money-savers as well as revenue-increasers. Why do the simple, little, cheap things not get done in marketing? I finally figured it out. They don't get done *because* they cost too little. Important managers spend their time making important decisions, and important decisions are decisions that cost the company lots of money. Average managers make decisions that cost average money; no managers make decisions that cost no money. There is no place on the budget for things that cost no money. That is the explanation.

I was in charge of a several-days session for a large real estate developer in China to allocate about US$3 million in promotion spending for Shanghai. One of the budget items was billboards. One billboard along Shanghai's major highway costs about $500,000 per year. The marketing manager proposed to advertise on four such billboards. I swear that there was a sense of accomplishment in the room as we all realized that this expense would take care of $2 million of the $3 million to be spent. We felt productive. Here is what I did that you should do your next marketing meeting when you decide on how and where to spend your budget. Don't start with the big items. First assign this great question to your managers: what suggestions do you have that cost no money?

*What suggestions do you have that cost no money?*

It would be good if companies could start defining important things as things that *make* the company lots of money. For example, sales for a roach-killer product sold mostly in independent hardware stores multiplied many-fold if the product was put on the counter near the cash register. Victory or defeat was achieved in the sales conversation between storeowner and sales representative, with the product ending up on the counter or on the shelf.

Here was one small thing that was the one big thing the marketing manager for this product should become a total expert on and manage to perfection. He or she should go on sales calls to educate him- or herself and to search for ways to improve the batting averages. For example, the independent hardware storeowners and managers are almost exclusively older men. Perhaps an effective and attractive female salesperson might be extra successful in getting the product on the store counter? Perhaps a higher margin or upfront cash payment for the stores that put the product on the counter would help? The marketing manager should not wonder about such things; he or she should experiment and then take advantage of the findings.

I thought this was an extremely exciting and important finding, a key leverage point crying out for experimentation and management to perfection. But I don't remember that my enthusiasm was shared at all by the company. I wasn't a consultant to the company, just a Ph.D. student who happened to know some of the managers. But I don't think that was why my excitement was ignored. I think the top managers, the marketing manager, the advertising manager, the finance manager, the CEO; they all were too busy, talking to one another about the product, the label, the advertisement, the advertising budget, the marketing plan, financing, hiring more people, and so on. We get so busy managing, we forget the business. When it's all over we wake up and try to figure out what the heck we were thinking.

> *Don't be so busy managing that you forget to find and keep great customers.*

Do you know the key leverage points in your business, and do you manage them to perfection? Most likely they are somewhere outside your business. Our soldiers, the people near the bottom of the pyramid, people so low in the hierarchy they actually talk to customers; these people often wonder what it is that top management is thinking, what it is that they are doing all day.

Here is a little secret. Top management sometimes doesn't know either. They go to meetings, give speeches, sit in on presentations. They run around, keeping very busy, not sure at all what to do. They haven't seen the market. They haven't touched any customers. Besieged, not making their numbers, they retreat into their offices and cut spending here and there or do a merger or something.

Many companies could use more of what I call the Donna attitude. By 1993, Donna had motorcycled around the United States for long enough and decided to settle down in New Orleans. So she bought a bar on the edge of the French quarter. She paid next to nothing because the bar, now called Donna's Bar and Grill, was next to nothing, literally. This was a street the locals knew to avoid, and out-of-towners wouldn't know to find. So she came to an advertising class I was teaching at the time to get some free advice on how to advertise; one important constraint being that there was no money for advertising.

One suggestion I made was to have someone in an alligator costume roam the main tourist area in the French quarter some six blocks away and hand out coupons for free beers (not the old discount coupons) together with a menu showing various alligator dishes. Renting the suit and printing the coupons and menus was not expensive. In a day or two of trial, Donna could *see* if it worked with less effort than it would take to sit around in the bar and *debate* whether it would work.

As it turned out, the idea worked very well. People didn't walk six blocks to drink just one beer and then walk back. Once she had found her lever, Donna didn't let go. You sometimes only need one simple thing; then you need to do it. Ten years later, Donna's (www.donnasbarandgrill.com) has become popular with music lovers worldwide for that unique in-your-face New Orleans brass jazz that, as Donna says, makes you jump up and down and shout "WE ROLLIN'!!". Sometimes I'm proud to be a marketing professor.

It is good to plan carefully. But be careful that the plan that keeps you busy does not stop you from asking and answering the most important questions. Who do we want as customers? Where and how do we find and keep those customers?

Let me close this book, then, by reiterating key points I made in different ways throughout this book: Let me call it a Marketing Mea Culpa: say after me ...

> We are our worst enemy
> We love ourselves too much
> We know our customers too little
> We know too little about marketing
> We are too afraid to try out new things

We prefer to be busy inside our company
We forget to learn from companies anywhere
We forget our mission is to find and keep great customers

Too many managers spend too much time inside their companies, keeping up with their assigned responsibilities, trying to do what everybody else is doing. But ultimately, success is decided not inside our offices, not inside our company, not where we live our working life, not by us; but outside our company, by our customers, when and where they meet our product. There, where the rubber meets the road, is where we need to play, test, experiment, fail or succeed.

> *Success in marketing is achieved outside, not inside, the company.*

## ✍ POINTS TO REMEMBER

- ☞ Build and maintain an organization chart showing all players involved in moving your product.
- ☞ Everyone who influences the success of your product, directly or indirectly, should be treated as a valued customer.
- ☞ When you help your channel, you help yourself.
- ☞ Do the little things right; big things take care of themselves.
- ☞ Manage your stores.
- ☞ If you steal from your friends, how many friends will you have?
- ☞ Add value throughout the value chain. Worry first about your customers' business model.
- ☞ Solving your customers' problems solves your problems.
- ☞ Sophisticated formulas don't help when you put in the wrong numbers.
- ☞ Maximizing your customers' profits maximizes your profits.
- ☞ Don't be the Louisiana Office of Motor Vehicles.
- ☞ What suggestions do you have that cost no money?
- ☞ Don't be so busy managing that you forget to find and keep great customers.
- ☞ Success in marketing is achieved outside, not inside, the company.

# Notes

1. Susan Greco, "When is it Safe to Hire? How One Group of CEOs Got Past Their Fear of Hiring Salespeople," *Inc.* (January 2007), pp. 52–3. See also the interview with Taylor MacDonald, Enterprise Resource VP for Sage Software: "Helping Partners," *eWeek*, http://www.esp.eweek.com/article/Helping+Partners/186894_1.aspx
2. M.V. Marn and R.L. Rosiello, "Managing Price, Gaining Profit," *Harvard Business Review* (September/October 1992).
3. Susanne Klingner and Rainer Stadler, "Der Spion Der Aus Der Kalte Kam," *Suddeutsche Zeitung Magazin* (30 January 2007), pp. 9–11.
4. Roopa Umashankar and Sumit Kumar Chaudhuri, "Progressive Corp: The Auto Insurer's Competitive Strategies," *ICFAI Business School Case Development Centre*, 2004.
5. Ray Kroc, *Grinding it Out: The Making of Mcdonald's* (St. Martin's Paperbacks,1992), p. 84.
6. The early history of Brightstar is described in "Closing the Deal" by Christopher McDougall, *Inc.* (March 2004), pp. 72–84.
7. See www.brightstarcorp.com
8. The National Committee for Quality Assurance, "The State of Managed Care Quality," Washington, D.C., October 1998.
9. See ihi.org for a list of supporters. Also ask your hospital if it participates in the IHI program.
10. Visit ihi.org for details.
11. Bo Burlingham, "Building a Marketing Juggernaut,"*Inc.* (November 2003), pp. 58–67.

# Postscript

I end the book abruptly because that is my style – like the trumpeter of Krakow, silenced in mid-note by an enemy arrow. Less poetic is "because the rule of show business is to always leave them wanting more."

Additionally, if the book gets any thicker, probably fewer people will read it. Education is a business where people generally prefer to get a little less rather than a little more. Looking at the wildly successful, *Who Moved My Cheese?* I think I probably already wrote far too much.

I do hope and trust though that you didn't just enjoy the book, but that you found enough worthwhile ideas to unleash your inner marketing genius, to make yourself and your company more successful and more profitable, starting today. This is really your job here – to identify and act on the particular points I made that are most relevant to you and your company.

So bring your company that "Donna attitude": learn from anybody. Experiment and have fun. Love your product, your customers, and your marketing. And if things are not working, just keep experimenting until the market starts jumping, and you start shouting "WE ROLLIN'!!".

Thank you for your attention.

# Index